Behind the Veil: My Journey with a "Prophet"

From Brooklyn to Beautiful!

He has made everything *beautiful* in its time. He has also set eternity in the human heart; yet no one can fathom what God has done from beginning to end.

Ecclesiastes 3:11

By Diane Y. Jones Gardner

From Brooklyn to Beautiful!

Behind the Veil: My Journey with a "Prophet"

From Brooklyn to Beautiful

Copyright © 2020 by Diane Y. Jones Gardner

Published 2020 by Book baby www.bookbaby.com

First Edition

Printed in the United States of America

ISBN # 978-1-09832-788-0

Dedications

This book is dedicated to my family—my loving Husband Victor who gave me space and peace to work on myself and this book. You saw beautiful in me before I saw it in myself. I love you more than words could ever say. To my children—Kevin, Nefertiti, Alexander, and Genesis; my desire and drive to be my very best are because of you and for you. I am because you all are my beautiful children!

I also dedicate this book to my five-year-old self. You are beautiful! From your curly, coarse hair and your shiny dark brown eyes to your perched pouting lips. I wish I could have told you back then all that I know about you today. I want you to know that I love you! I couldn't tell you or show you that but know that you have grown into a powerful, beautiful, courageous woman of God! Everything you endured was not in vain!

Table of Contents

Prologue

The Journey begins…

As I was attempting to put together all of the many notes, journal entries, prayers, and encounters that I have experienced over the course of my journey, I struggled to make sense of how this should flow. Where I should start and what I should include. It is my belief that God heard my silent frustration and intervened…

Encounter 5:30 a.m.: This morning when I woke up I saw a vision of a veil that stood between me and God; I was a child standing in front of the veil, looking from its top to the bottom, puzzled, trying to figure out how to remove it! Then God spoke to me. He said, *"TAKE YOUR JOURNEY BACK TO THE BEGINNING."* I said, "Do you mean my childhood?" God said, *"NO, FROM THE MOMENT YOU STOOD BEHIND THE VEIL!"*

God then took me back to when he first spoke these words to me—October 20, 2014, He gently said to me, *"YOU ARE STILL RUNNING! EVERYTHING YOU HAVE BEEN*

THROUGH, ALL OF THE TRIALS YOU HAVE EXPERIENCED WERE NOT IN VAIN. THEY WERE TO GET YOU CLOSER TO ME. YOU GOT RIGHT OUTSIDE OF THE VEIL AND YOU STOPPED MOVING! MY DESIRE IS FOR YOU TO TEAR THROUGH AND EXPERIENCE THE FULL DEPTH OF MY SPIRIT AND MY POWER. I WANT TO USE YOU IN WAYS LIKE NEVER BEFORE. BUT YOU MUST BREAK THROUGH! THIS IS NOT THE TIME TO GET COMPLACENT, FEARFUL, OR DISTRACTED, OR TO TURN BACK! I NEED YOU, BUT MOST IMPORTANTLY YOU NEED ME! YOU ARE MORE THAN EQUIPPED BECAUSE "I AM." STOP DOUBTING ME; I DO NOT NEED YOUR SKILL OR YOUR PERMISSION, I NEED YOUR WILLINGNESS AND I WILL DO THE REST. MY DAUGHTER, FEAR NOT… COME TO ME, COME"!!! (2 Corinthians 3:12-18)

Transparency: *Tearfully I thought to myself, I KNOW I have been running… more so I am racked with the feelings of inadequacy, doubt, and fear. Who am I? Why me? So I've been moving in mediocrity; KNOWING and feeling that I am supposed to be doing more! Not out of conceit, worthiness, or arrogance but out of this overwhelming urge to break out of my own skin! I literally feel the struggle between my spirit and my flesh. My spiritual man is wrestling and fighting for my life and I am doing nothing about it out of fear…. (God help me!) Prayerfully confessing this will free me from the grips of fear and take the veil off of my eyes!

As I reminisced on this encounter from 2014, I got up, grabbed my book, went into my quiet space, and began to write!!!! God gave me the backdrop of what I needed to share with you (transparency, struggles, confessions, lessons and testimonies)!!! Everything else will be my communication and the step-by-step instructions (from A Prophet) that I took to remove the veil! I pray that my experiences will encourage you to face your own veils and TEAR THEM DOWN!

As I was writing, God said to me, *"WHAT ARE THE VEILS IN YOUR LIFE?"* I had to think back to what I knew about how God dealt with me on this journey: fear, timidity, debt, dysfunctional marriage, lack of peace, broken relationship with God, and being disconnected from His Source! I had to write down everything that blocked my purpose and I had to be honest about it...What I discovered through this journey is that you will only go as far as your honesty will take you! As much as we want to believe that a Prophet can tell us all about our past, present, and future, the truth of the matter is that even if God gives them insight into the deepest and darkest places in our lives, we still have the power of "denial." And once we deny the truth, the lesson is over and the journey ends! Scriptures tell us that you shall know the truth and the truth will set you free (**John 8:32**)! When we get sick and tired of being stuck, stuck in the wilderness of self-pity, fear, and doubt and tired of being a slave to sin and the flesh, eventually, we will find ourselves standing in front of our "veil" begging God to do anything to remove it! What God had to show me was that the veil didn't even exist (**Matthew 27:50, 51**); it represented my own limited perception of who I believed He was and what I believed he could do!

This book, *Behind the Veil: My Journey with "A Prophet" from Brooklyn to Beautiful*, will take you on a trip with me to experience healing, deliverance, faith, and blessings! I do not profess to be a preacher, a teacher, a prophet, or a bible scholar, nor is this book about pericopes or exegesis. This is strictly a book about my personal relationship and experiences with the Almighty Living God! I cannot speak for anyone else, only for myself; however, I know that someone somewhere can identify and relate to some of the challenges I faced on my journey. Walk with me as I navigate my way through this thing called LIFE!

✠✠✠

Behind The Veil!

Chapter I: Brooklyn State of Mind!

God asked me, "WHAT DOES BROOKLYN REPRESENT TO YOU?" I said, "My past relationship with Him!"

Brooklyn, NY, is where I was born and raised; my memories are of brick homes, landscaped high-risers, walking across the Brooklyn Bridge, adventurous train ride including the most talented panhandlers the world had "never" seen, ma and pa, shops where everyone knew the who's who in the neighborhood, Hollywood lights, Harlem St. (the Apollo Theater), 42nd Street movie strip where the adult films fought the $2 horror flick for your attention, glitz, and glamour on an intense budget—one of the richest, diverse, busy, and beautiful fun places you could ever want to live in. Where the city never sleeps and opportunities knock down your door, begging you to shine your bright light on them! But for me Brooklyn represented the familiar and the comfortable; a place where I felt stuck in my environment with no way out, feeling like I had a deeper purpose but not knowing how to obtain it! I had been in this place often—constricted, scared, uncertain, feeling inadequate, ugly, and ashamed. Nothing within me told me that

I was important or worthy enough to remove what I used as a covering to block myself from the presence of God. Why was I hiding? Why didn't I see myself as beautiful? (Let us fast forward.)

11/17/2019 8:00 p.m.: As I sat at this conference I was helping to facilitate as Worship Leader, entitled "Let it Burn with the Holy Ghost Fire," I was so far removed from that actual feeling of the Holy Ghost Fire! I couldn't recall the last time I heard and listened to God's comforting voice. I had been a frequent faster, prayer warrior; I saw visions, dreamed dreams, interpreted spiritual language; I was on FIRE for Christ! Nothing could shake my faith. If I had an issue, I knew exactly who to take it to, and although there were times of complacency and sometimes chaos in my life, my heart was always at peace, until it happened. In 2015, I was carjacked at gunpoint while sitting in my car waiting for my son to get off work! I heard a knock on my car window, as I turned to face who I thought was my son; I stared down the barrel of a handgun! As the assailant yelled "GET OUT OF THE CAR," I screamed and opened my door, and as I stood up I could see the eyes of a scared child through the mask I faced; nothing in me told me to pray, call on the Lord, or even speak to this wounded soul as he nervously pointed this gun in my direction. In order for him to get in my car, we actually brushed up against each other so that I could get past and let him drive away with my car, my pocketbook, my house keys and my courage! I felt as if something was transferred from him to me in our exchange because at that very moment I felt like he looked—terrified. I lost so much more than my possessions that day. I lost my life as I once knew it! I feared everything!!!! You see, something triggered inside of me… this was not the first time I encountered a gun. Back in my 20s, I was shot in the stomach in my own home. I had a private birthday party for a friend and someone (who I believe) was attempting to come in to rob my guests. They knocked on the door and when I went to look through the peephole, I saw someone with a black mask on. I believed it was a joke until I heard a POP! They shot through the door hitting me at close range in my abdomen! I didn't believe I was shot so I struggled to walk; it was dark and the music was loud. No one at the party even realized what happened. As I limped from person to person, faintly whispering "I think I got shot," one of my cousins could finally interpret what I was saying. He shouted, "TURN THE MUSIC OFF!!!" The music was turned off, the lights turned up, and I hit the floor! As I laid on the ground believing that I would die at any moment (because I could feel the fire of the bullet traveling through my body and feared the fragments would hit a vital organ), I prayed to the Lord, "God if you let me live, I promise I will serve you. Please don't let me die!" At that time I had two children, my four-year-old son and my two-year-old baby girl. I couldn't leave them motherless. I just kept seeing their faces in my mind as I pleaded with God to let me survive this thing. Well, I survived it; God kept his promise and although I forfeited my oath many times over, God was faithful and just forgave me of my sins, and cleansed me of all unrighteousness. And seven years later, I was baptized at 8 p.m. that evening. By 12 midnight I boarded a train from Brooklyn, NY, to Atlanta, GA, and I never looked back!!!

So here I was sitting at this conference, three years after the carjacking incidence, praying this would not be like any other event where I would have a zeal and get all pumped up only to leave exhausted; where I would dance, shout, and jump around from the "feeling" of God's presence without even recognizing when he enters the room; where I would get all filled up only to be hungry again…. That this would not be an event in which after all of the hooting and hollering I would go home just to stare back up at my veil! But I could tell, there was something different or should I say someone different at this conference. You see it's never just about who we meet in life but it is about paying attention to those divine connections; those people and relationships that God preordained for us. The ones predestined to direct us to our purpose and destiny! I'm not talking about meeting new friends or networking, I'm not even talking about meeting someone who would become a spouse or reconnecting with a long-lost relative but meeting someone intertwined with our lives strictly for the purpose of connecting us to God! This begins my journey with "the Prophet"…. I call him "PC"!

Chapter II: Divine Connection!

What is the purpose and importance of a prophet in your life? *I will raise up for them a prophet like you from among their fellow Israelites, and I will put my words in his mouth. He will tell them everything I command him* (**Deuteronomy 18:18**). The Lord used a prophet to bring Israel up from Egypt, by a prophet he cared for him (**Hosea 12:13**).

~ When you trust and obey the words of a Prophet, you Profit!

2 Chronicles 20:20 ~

A Prophet(ess) is the mouthpiece of God! A man or woman of God who speaks by divine inspiration or as the interpreter through whom the Will of God is expressed. They are the bridge between where you are and where God wants to take you! Now I am no stranger to the works of a Prophet; for some strange reason, God saw fit to surround me with friends and family members who are pastors, ministers, prophetess, bishops, elders, and the likes thereof. I have participated in prayer meetings where demonic spirits have been exposed and literally cast out! I've seen the mighty hand of God move and felt his undeniable presence and yet I still reside behind the veil!

So why would I feel like this would be any different? I discovered the difference was God wasn't looking for me to "FEEL." He was looking for me to walk by faith and not by sight; to see if I would Trust Him! In **John 20:29**, Jesus told "doubting" Thomas after he had to see and feel the wombs of the Lord: you believed because you saw me but blessed are those who have not seen me, yet they believe. God is looking for serious folks who will trust him at his word, no matter what they feel and no matter what things look like. This journey with PC helped me to discover the areas in my life that would change FOREVER!!!!

Now I would be remiss if I didn't mention that in the beginning, I was a "skeptic" or should I say a "doubting" Diane, not because of anything I witnessed from PC but because I am very protective of my spirit, and the scripture tells us in **1 John 4:1**: *test the spirits to see whether they are from God because many false prophets have gone out into the world.*

So it was good to meet PC doing what he does in his element… During the prayer conference my daughter and I attended, I was called to come up to the front by PC to receive a prophetic word from the Lord. As PC spoke, in my mind I was like, "OK, what he is speaking is truth." After he spoke, I was then ushered over to a woman who accompanied him so she could pray over me. She prayed, blew in my right ear, and I hit the floor! I could vaguely hear but mostly I couldn't move (*God had arrested me!*). At this time, I believe he was speaking blessings over my daughter's life. I have no clue what was being said but when I got up and joined them and he realized I was her mother, he had shared with me that God spoke to him and he was to become my daughter's Godfather! He spoke of her character and how God was proud of her, and that he was to walk with her, myself, and her step dad to ensure that she would experience all that God had for her life! But it wasn't until we were about to leave when he asked her one simple question. He asked her, "How is your relationship with your biological dad?" With tears welling up in her eyes and a nervous smile on her face, she began to answer. Now, this was a rhetorical question because God had already revealed the answer to him so he stopped her before she unraveled and told her, "I already know... no matter what, you still make sure to love and respect him." He hugged her and told her, "God has blessed you to have a spiritual Godfather now and I will be here for you for, whatever you need!" He was genuine in his speech to her; he spoke directly and sincerely from the heart. It was at that very moment God blessed me with His "divine connection."

✠✠✠

Chapter III: Preparation

During our first phone consultation, I was asked by PC, "What three areas do you believe you need improvement in?"

My Response:"My three areas of concern are Faith, Finances, and Family

Faith: I know there is so much more God wants to do in me and through me but I need to conquer fear and walk in boldness!

Finances: Once upon a time I was debt-free but I allowed myself to go back into debt. So a lot of my finances are tied up in paying bills. I am climbing out slowly but have to become disciplined in ALL areas including giving. I become so over passionate about helping that I end up hurting myself. I am learning the difference between being a blessing, being an enabler, being taken advantage of, or being someone's God...."

Family: (1) My marriage has always been my biggest and most vulnerable area of attack because my husband and I are on different levels. He is more business orientated; I am more spiritual; if they can be combined it would be powerful. (2) My children were all given to God at birth and I see their spiritual greatness in the faith so I keep praying for their protection against entities and for their purpose to be manifested. But as they get older and become adults and start making their own decisions (good, bad, and indifferent), my fear increases due to the lack of control I have over them and the lack of trust I have in God to honor my prayers!

PC: This process will encompass obedience, commitment, focus and avoidance of distractions! Distractions have caused us to miss opportunities; opportunities are blessings!

But remember the LORD your God, for it is he who gives you the ability to produce wealth, and so confirms his covenant, which he swore to your ancestors, as it is today.

 (**Deuteronomy 8:18**). Seize every opportunity provided to you to obtain what is rightfully YOURS!

PC: What takes up your time? Write a list of things that occupy your time.

My List:

-Social Media

-Television

-Ministries

-Work

-Household obligations

PC: I want you to follow these instructions. Take an index card and place it on the right side of the refrigerator and on the wall in your bedroom at eye level after writing the following on it:

Diane is going to reroute her time!

Challenge: come up with a schedule that you will be dedicated to in order to do the following: Prayer, Mentoring Call, and Study

Prayer: Monday (mentoring call), Wednesday, and Friday

Studying: Tuesday, Thursday, and Saturday

PC: During Prayer and Meditation listen for God's voice, allow him to speak to you, and write down what he says. Spend at least thirty minutes each day around the same time. At the time you indicate, I will be praying and interceding on your behalf regarding what God says to me about you. It is my desire that you obtain all that God has for you!

I've always known the effects of writing things down but I had forgotten the power of repetition. When you get a declaration deep down in your spirit and you begin to see yourself walking

that thing out! It is freeing!!!

✠✠✠

Chapter IV: Fear Talks, Faith Walks!

Lesson I: Faith—Remove Fear and Trust God More

PC: Fine-tuning your faith means you are willing to endure the trials that come to strengthen your faith. Increasing your faith means being uncomfortable.

I confessed at this time that I walked in the spirit of timidity and fear.

I was instructed to write on index cards and stick them all over my house: the left side and right side of the mirrors, refrigerator, and bedroom door.

*I, Diane Yvette Gardner, will walk in BOLDNESS!

*My BOLDNESS is going to be challenged and I will accept the challenge!

I don't know why but for some reason I felt a shift immediately and I began to walk in BOLDNESS!

As it was spoken and as I also knew it would happen, when I said "YES" to change, the challenges started coming. How many of us know that there are no new tricks from that clown the devil; just different illusions! This one weapon had been formed against me for over a decade and I was ready for God to put it to REST! Without giving the darkness too much exposure I will keep this account discreet! There's a period in my life where I experienced abuse—verbal, physical, mental, and psychological. Most people don't recognize abuse until it becomes physical and by then you've already been held prisoner by the psychological effects of the verbal and emotional abuse: these characteristics are fear, low self-esteem, suicidal thoughts, despair, depression, anxiety, and helplessness! You become paralyzed by your own fear of being killed or wanting to kill yourself! The echoes of tormenting words spoken to you when they lose control of their control! "If I can't have you no one else will!" "I don't give a"f**k" about either one of our lives; I'll take us both out!" Threats, intimidating speech, erratic hand, and arm gestures. When Satan learns how to activate fear in you, he will use the most aggressive tactics that prove to work! I know that I am not fighting against the actual person but against principalities, against powers, against the rulers of the darkness of this world, against spiritual wickedness in high places (**Ephesians 6:12**). So here I am forced to face my past and my fears.

As my past resuscitated itself out of the dead womb in my life, I was abruptly approached by my adult son who out of desperation wanted to know why I was keeping this ugly "secret" from him. You see he didn't understand why I didn't have a healthy co-parenting relationship or why there were no kumbaya (harmonious) moments that he could pull out of his memory bank between our "broken family." As a parent, you feel like you have to protect your children's emotions by keeping sin "hidden." It never dawns on you that doing this very thing could repeat the cycle. My logic was I didn't want to paint an ugly picture in their mind about something they were not at home to witness or about someone they loved. It was embarrassing, demeaning, and traumatizing, so I buried it and continued to survive for the sake and sanity of protecting my children's "wholeness." But at that moment my son was broken! His heart, and his emotions, he was torn between the loyalty of one parent and the love of the other. And I felt every bit of the helplessness I felt when I was in the relationship! I can remember these piercing words he said to me, with tears streaming down his face, "PLEASE tell me what happened to you? I need to know why at times I have a short temper and uncontrolled anger!" That was it!!! This generational curse was NOT going any further!!!

A Mother's Prayer: Oh God, have mercy on my soul! Daddy, I lift my children up to you; I break every chain, every emotional tie, every elusive and vile spirit on assignment against my children. I bind the spirit of abuse, physical, mental, emotional, psychological, verbal, and the likes thereof. I cast out every stronghold designed to mask itself as love and affection! Devil, you can't have my children!!! Oh God, you said in your word "Even the captives of the mighty shall be taken away, And the prey of the terrible be delivered;

For I will contend with him who contends with you, And I will save your children. **(Isaiah 49:25)** God, I thank you for your word and your promise. I am not a perfect parent and I did my best to try and protect them from my choices but I feel like I FAILED!!! Daddy, I need you! I need you to repair the broken places, repair those areas that are damaged due to ME! God, help me to help my son! In Jesus' name, I pray. Amen!

God's Response: *MY PRECIOUS DAUGHTER, I AM THE LIVING GOD! I AM IN CONTROL OF EVERYTHING THAT PERTAINS TO YOU. TASTE AND SEE THE LORD IS GOOD. STAY AT MY FEET AND WATCH THE SALVATION OF THE LORD! I WILL DEAL WITH YOUR SON'S CONCERNS AND I WILL DEAL WITH YOU. I LOVE YOU AND I HAVE YOUR BEST INTEREST AT HEART. DO NOT WORRY OR FEAR. TRUST ME, STAND ON MY WORD AND NO MATTER WHAT THINGS LOOK LIKE, YOU WILL NOT FAIL! I AM THE LORD, YOUR GOD, AND I WILL HONOR EVERYTHING CONCERNING YOU! I KNOW WHAT WORRIES YOU, I KNOW WHAT YOU HAVE BEEN DEALING WITH FOR SO MANY YEARS. GIVE IT TO ME! THIS BATTLE WAS NEVER DESIGNED FOR YOU TO FIGHT, ONLY TO WAIT ON ME, ONLY TO SEEK ME FOR GUIDANCE, AND ONLY TO BEHOLD AS I FIGHT THIS BATTLE FOR YOU. I AM PATIENTLY WAITING FOR YOU TO FINALLY GIVE IT TO ME ONCE AND FOR ALL. DO NOT FRET OVER THIS; I HAVE ALWAYS KEPT YOU THROUGH IT. IT WAS DESIGNED TO ATTACK YOU BUT*

NEVER TO HARM YOU. YOU MUST RISE ABOVE FEAR, THE CLAMOR, THE OVER THINKING, THE ANGER, THE WORRY, AND GIVE THIS DISTRACTION TO ME! I WILL SHOW YOU ONCE AND FOR ALL HOW I DEAL WITH THIS. IT IS A DISTRACTION! I GOT YOU! (**2 Chronicles 20:15**).

God gave me five steps to help me in this process using Psalm 62:1-12

1—Acknowledge who God is to me! Verses 1 and 2

2—Deal with the assault, call it out! Verses 3 and 4

3—Don't stay dwelling on the offender, remind myself again who God is and what He can do! Verses 5–7

4—Trust HIM and tell others why they should trust Him! Verses 8–10

5—Talk directly to God! Tell Him what you heard about his power and His love! Speak His promises back to Him! Verse 11 and 12

I cannot tell you that this delivered me from fear, but my fighting technique did change!

To PC (8:00 a.m.): This morning I kept giving my concerns to God but I kept seeing my son in my mind break down in an emotional state as I kept rehearsing my defense in my head. Even after I gave it to God it was a HUGE distraction!!! But while driving to work, I kept snapping out of it, taking captive every thought and praising God, talking even louder to him about His promises than my thoughts were trying to talk to me about my problem. And before I knew it, I was speaking in tongues saying every one of my children's names out loud, and all of a sudden I began praying in English with BOLDNESS Casting EVERY demon back to hell, every root, and tentacle. I believe it was the translation of what was spoken in tongues because the prayer was SO different and forceful! By the time I finished, my heart was at peace and my mind stable. Good, God!!!! It was AWESOME, and God excitedly said to me, *"THAT'S HOW YOU FIGHT! I GOT THIS! VENGEANCE IS MINE!"* Hallelujah!!! I know the battle is not over but God already won this war....

PC: I'm extremely Proud of You! See it's one thing to react out of Fear but when you Fight with BOLDNESS, you are prepared to take a few licks because in your mind and Spirit you know YOU'RE GOING TO WIN THE FIGHT!! I want you to consider Allowing the Truth to be told to your Son, at least as much Truth as he can handle because The Truth Shall Free Him from the hold that is on him! Now all you have to begin to do is Walk and React in BOLDNESS KNOWING THAT NO MATTER WHAT HE DOES OR SAYS, GOD HAS TOLD YOU HE'S GOT YOU.

*I revealed my truth to my son; of course, it was disputed but none of that mattered, I was FREE and my son was now able to understand why his mother's heart beats the way it does. You see, because of this hidden sin my son could never understand why there wasn't a functioning relationship, why I couldn't be in the same space as my offender, or why I showed fear in my demeanor whenever they were around. Make no mistake, I forgave him a long time ago; I HAD TO. But forgiving someone does not stop the offense. I forgave so that I wouldn't take my anger out on my children and so that I was free to love again! GLORY!!

If I had to sum up the lesson I learned on faith walking, I would have to say this was a milestone; this was my David and Goliath moment! You see there were several smaller steps I took by faith that catapulted me to the main battle. My prayer life changed, my studies gave me power, and my giving/sowing seed opened up a level of trust for God that enabled me to face my fears and carry out the things I was instructed to do. I cannot say that I will not have to face this giant again but what I do know is that MY God is bigger than ANY mountain, giant, man, woman, fear, or foe I could ever face!!! And I am coming BOLDLY with my sling and stones! (**1 John 4:4**).

✠✠✠

Chapter V: Finances: Funny Money
Poem: *You Got Jokes*!

I sit here as I listen to the laughter of the change jingling in my purse

But the joke is on me as I struggle to pay late fees while things get

worse

-My money is funny and I am not laughing

Do you hear it mocking me? Telling me I cannot afford to pay

attention?

As I put all of my trust into the stock market and now I have no

pension

-My money is telling me jokes and I am not laughing

Checks, Cash, and Good Credit all walking out the door with

Prosperity and Success

Debt, Bills, and High blood pressure got me walking around here

with all this Stress!

-My money is a real comedian and I am not laughing

Knock, knock, who's there? It's not your money… hahaha

Stimulus checks, bailout agreements, real funny… blah blah blah

-My money's hilarious but I am not laughing

Money, the earth is the Lord's and everything in it too, so who's

your owner?

I am in Christ, which makes me an heir of you; not a borrower but a

donor

So who's laughing now? Chuckle giggle laugh laugh

My trust is in the Lord so the wicked is storing you up, on MY

behalf…Chi Chang! ©DJG 09/29/08

LEAP: *A leap of faith, in its most commonly used meaning, is the act of believing in or accepting something outside the boundaries of reason.*

Lesson 2: Financial Freedom—The List!

PC: What are you willing to sacrifice? What are you willing to release to God?

*Credit Cards/DEBT! This is my crutch in between pay cycles etc. Cut them up, get out of debt, no more spending only sowing!

*Purge Clothes closet; bless someone with the excess; only keep what I currently wear.

*FEAR; got to go!!! I will not allow fear to block any more blessings; if God provides an opportunity and fear is my first reaction, I AM LEAPING!!! God has not given me a spirit of fear! (**2 Timothy 1:7**).

*Pride: being right/believing I am the only one who knows what God wants and needs for this family! (Whew! transparency lol) I will trust my husband with the decisions he makes (good, bad, or indifferent). I will pray and not question (trust GOD to do what's needed in him) and encourage from the HEART. He is the head of our household, and I will let him be that in whatever way he shows it, and God will elevate him to his rightful position!!! GLORY!

*Sons: let them stand on their own two feet; if they can't, let them figure it out just like I did! Genesis is my focus! Have the tough talk with them about their future and me and my husband's plans and stick to it! Give them a realistic timeline to get stable so that they can support themselves.

Entertainment: outside of whatever is already paid for, cut back on spending on trips! Keep it simple.

Stop trying to carry the load! Get out of debt and stay out; ask my husband for help! Stop pretending that (1) I don't need his financial support and (2) I can do it all! Tackle one project at a time, get his financial support, and keep it simple!

Characteristics I see in all of this that WILL be purged:

Pride (being right)

Gluttony (excess)

Fear (timidity, low self-esteem)

Insecurity (debt)

Control (sons, husband)

Lack of trust (in God and in husband)

THIS WAS HARD and made me very vulnerable!!!!! But I am trusting that God will hold my hand every step of the way as I leap!

PC: WOW! Let me just say I'm extremely Proud of you for being Honest with yourself and being Transparent! Most importantly for Allowing yourself to become vulnerable and Trusting That God Will Protect You!! Now as far as the Credit Cards are concerned, don't cut them yet. They will be cut on the last day of the year. Blessing someone with your Overflow is a Great way to keep your Blessings flowing!! Every time you take a LEAP it Increases your FAITH and removes your FEAR!! And the More You Leap the Less FEAR you'll have because every time you LEAP God releases MANIFESTATIONS which makes it easier to LEAP!! Pride now, that's a BIGGIE because that takes a CHANGE of MINDSET! That also requires you to constantly remind yourself that it's not about You, which brings you to becoming HUMBLE! Releasing your Sons is a TRUE ACT OF LOVE!! Allowing them to Grow and Develop into MEN! Also when you RELEASE them into God's Hands, He is Responsible for their Growth and Well-being!! Entertainment—Everyone needs some Entertainment at some point as long as you don't overextend yourself trying to be ENTERTAINED, and besides your husband probably enjoys doing special things with you. Now finally asking your husband for help is Wise because he probably has the means to pull you out but you have to come CLEAN WITH HIM!! Share with him how you got in this situation and APOLOGIZE for Allowing this to become a Situation in your Family!!! Yes, that means EAT CROW!! LOL, this will also allow Humility to work within you and help Diminish your PRIDE!!

To PC (9:38 a.m.): Where do I start? Yesterday I confessed to you something that I've NEVER confessed to anyone (not even GOD)! My instructions from you were to confess my debt/spending habits to my husband and watch the hand of God move on my behalf, freeing me from bondage, releasing those spirits from my life, and creating an atmosphere in which my husband can take his rightful place on his throne and me on mine. ALL 100 percent TRUTH!!! ALL day I fretted over this thing. How would I tell him? When would I tell him? Will he be too tired to really listen? How will he react? I even played that thing out in my mind with him embracing me for being honest, vulnerable, and endearing OR him being devastated and angry with me and not speaking to me for days! I spoke with him by phone several times throughout the day to ensure he would DROP everything and come home because "we need to talk" where he would nervously ask "So what do we need to talk about?" (Every man's reaction before putting themselves in the line of fire of a woman's emotions.... lol.) I came home early, called to let him know I was home and to see if he would be able to once again drop everything and come home. He had tows backed up as usual in the winter…. I begin to worry that it's not going to happen! It has to happen TONIGHT, I thought! I started praying to God, "PLEASE allow my husband to come home so that we can talk and I can confess this thing!" God said to me: *MY PRECIOUS DAUGHTER, I LOVE YOU AND NOTHING CAN SEPARATE YOU FROM MY LOVE, NOT DEATH, LIFE, ANGELS, DEMONS, NOT MONEY, NOT DEBT, AND NOT EVEN YOUR HUSBAND! I KNOW ALL*

AND SEE ALL AND I HAVE THE POWER TO WIPE AWAY ANY DEBT, ANY TRANSGRESSION, AND ANY SIN. HOWEVER, YOU HAVE NOT EVEN CONFESSED TO ME!!! SEEK ME FOR HELP AND I WILL TURN HEARTS, BANK ACCOUNTS, DECISIONS, AND "I" WILL REVERSE CURSES AND RELEASE ABUNDANCE INTO YOUR LIFE! I AM YOUR GOD AND I KNOW EVERYTHING ABOUT YOU AND I STILL LOVE YOU JUST THE SAME. NOTHING CAN SEPARATE YOU FROM THAT LOVE...... THERE ARE THINGS THAT I NEED TO WORK OUT IN YOU BUT THERE ARE ALSO THINGS I NEED TO WORK OUT IN YOUR HUSBAND. I WILL NOT FORSAKE YOU, TRUST ME! STAY AT MY FEET, FEAR NOT, STAND FIRM AND SEE THE SALVATION OF THE LORD. (**Proverbs 28:13**) I don't need to tell you that I wept!!!! I confessed it ALL; 30,000-plus dollars' worth of debt to God! I repented, not just for getting into debt but for idolizing money and man! I cried some more and I asked him for help!

I don't know when this conversation will happen between my husband and me, but I trust and know that it WILL happen because secrets kill marriages. However, God knows him and how he is, so the groundwork has to be laid in HIM, now that he has worked in ME, and I forgot about the only one who is able to put in overtime on us both!

PC: Well Done! Yes, God is going to prepare his heart to Receive! Let me share with you why men hate hearing those few words, "We Need to Talk," because most women never have good news when they "want to talk," they only want our undivided attention when there's a problem, but it doesn't have to be that way in your marriage. You can make it so that when you say those words your husband will run to talk because he knows that you've got Good News to share!! Make your Marriage Atmosphere Different from the Norm!! Now that you've Confessed and Repented, how do you feel? Are you now ready to Make Serious and Aggressive Moves? Because when you confess to your husband, I need you to be ready as he's going to want to hear a Plan of Action!!

My Response: Absolutely! And you are so right; those words will forever be considered taboo as shown in movies, or real life, etc. But YES I do have the power to change that; I don't use them often but when either one of us uses them we almost always come ready to defend ourselves lol. I truly believe once I confess to him, I will open myself up to accountability! Currently, even though I should have been accountable to God, I wasn't. I spent what I wanted how I wanted and never had to be questioned because it was "MY" money and my DEBT and because I had a job to pay it off I never gave it a second thought. At this point, I made a plan but GOD'S plan will prevail (**Proverbs 16:9**).

Oh and I feel AWESOME!! Because even though I haven't faced the fiery furnace yet, lol, I now know I am not going in there alone and no matter how my husband receives it, I trust God to work it all out in the end!

PC: You're quickly becoming my prize pupil! Now, remember whatever his response is, you have to Receive it pleasantly and Humbly because the bottom line is you put you all in this predicament! But I believe if you put that defeated face on (lol) and don't get defensive, he'll shake his head, get a little heated, and then hug his wife and say we'll work it out! Now he's going to be a little skeptical because he's bailed you out before and now he has to do it again, but when you present him with the Cut Cards and your plan (that he has to approve), I believe he'll be more likely to want to believe that you have truly changed your spending habits.

I have since confessed to my husband; he was shocked and disappointed (as expected) but I could tell he was surprised that I had the guts to even confess it to him; nothing like what I was expecting!

The Jars (Luke 6:38)

PC (5:50 p.m.): Now the work begins. Follow these careful instructions: get a gallon of orange juice jar, clean it out, place $1.00 a day in it every day, $5.00 on the weekend, and $10.00 every payday for the entire month of December. Name the Jar "Seed 2018" and at the end of the month, you will present the jar to your husband to decide where you should sow your seed.

Write the following on index cards and place on the wall in your bedroom, bathroom, kitchen, and near the T.V:

*The Gardner family is DEBT FREE, Healthy, and prosperous!

*This family is WEALTHY (RICH)!

*I, Diane Yvette Gardner, will be aware of opportunities that God presents to me so that I might have multiple streams of income!

*I, Diane Yvette Gardner, will be a consistent giver so that my family can be a consistent harvester!

Every Month you will fill up your jar (January was Vision, February was LOVE, and March and April were for Victory) and at the end of every month, God will instruct on how your seed should be sown.

I was instructed to present my first jar to my husband and when I did, his first reaction was "PAY YOUR DEBT" (I chuckled). But God changed his heart and he instructed me instead to sow into our home church; he felt our church would use it to bless multiple families in need.

Praise Report: After sowing my seed on December 31st, God took me to the next level by thrusting me into the DEEP; I was placed on the Praise Team at my home church effective immediately (that same evening) and I received word of an increase in my salary at work!

Transparency: God gave me the desire and gift of singing and up until the end of 2018, I feared really using it! My desire to sing was getting bigger than my ability to do so because after going through the abuse I lost confidence in myself; I didn't like the sound of my own voice. You see when your cries are powerless and your voice is silenced, you neither have any belief that mountains can move nor do you hear any beauty in the sound you make! Now that I am on the Praise Team at my church, the expectation is much more demanding than being in the background hidden by all of the beautiful voices that surround me. My prayer and desire have ALWAYS been that I am not just a "pretty" voice but that God anoints my vocal cords so that when I open my mouth, healing, deliverance, and restoration takes place. But now that it's time to put faith into action, I believe my skill level is mediocre in comparison to others, so I find myself overcompensating, practicing and practicing for the songs we have to sing. The more I practice, the more off-tune I sound to myself; the more my voice becomes weaker, the more inadequate I feel. I would start belting out the songs, getting more and more frustrated because nothing I did made me feel comfortable enough to be at peace with how I was singing. I would begin to cry, telling God, "I want to do my best, I don't want to let you down." He said ever so gently, *"STOP THE PRESS... YES, I GAVE YOU THE GIFT OF SINGING AND YOU DO SOUND 'PRETTY' BUT IT IS NOT YOUR ABILITY THAT I WILL BE ANOINTING; IT IS YOUR INABILITY THAT I WILL TOUCH"! SING FOR ME! SING TO ME! PRAISE ME! EXALT ME!* This time as I opened my mouth and closed my eyes and begin singing directly to the Lord, I begin reminiscing on every blessing, His love, faithfulness, and His GRACE, and as I was singing effortlessly I began to understand it's neither about a degree, stature, practice, my skills nor is it about ME. Although all of those things require me to "study to show myself approved" when it comes to God's grace and anointing, you CANNOT earn it, learn it, or buy it, it is given. I am learning that God truly does use the foolish things we do to make the "wise" IN us humble **(1 Corinthians 1:27, 28)**.

Vision #1 (11:18 a.m.): As I lay on the floor worshiping and crying out to God, this is what I saw: I kept seeing this vision of myself as a little girl being carried in Daddy's arms. So secure, comfortable, and happy, but he put me down and bid me walk on my own two feet, urging me to move on. I kept looking back at him for surety and he would shake his head "yes" and nudge me along. As I walked further and further away, I still kept looking back to make sure he was still watching me. I begin to turn into a beautiful woman. This is what the Lord said to me: *MY DAUGHTER, YOU ARE MATURING INTO A BEAUTIFUL WOMAN; ONE WHO WILL WALK ON MY WORD AND IN MY WAYS. DO NOT FEAR. I WILL NEVER LEAVE YOU NOR FORSAKE YOU. I WILL ALWAYS GUIDE YOU ALONG YOUR WAY. CONTINUE TO LOOK TO ME, BUT NOW I AM RAISING YOU UP TO STAND AS A WOMAN OF GOD. YOU WILL ALWAYS BE MY CHILD, MY DAUGHTER, AND MY SPECIAL GEM. BUT YOU MUST PREPARE YOURSELF TO STAND ON FAITH AND TRUST THAT EVEN WHEN YOU ARE NOT IN MY ARMS, I AM ALWAYS PRESENT WITH YOU. YOU MUST BECOME INDEPENDENT AND STILL; SEEK ME OUT.> I love you Daddy. *MY DAUGHTER, I

KNOW YOU ARE FEARFUL TO WALK ON YOUR OWN BUT I AM WITH YOU ALWAYS. STAND TALL, WALK STRONG, AND DO MY WILL! (**1 Corinthians 13:11**).

Vision #2 (11:23 a.m.): I saw myself as this beautiful woman and as I walked away looking back at the Lord, I stopped and ran back into his arms, crying; he pushed me away extending my arms out and began to dance with me like a waltz. I moved as he moved; every step he took I took in unison. I began to smile with peace. Then we stopped and I ran off. I felt peace, joy, and confidence in my heart! I prayed out loud: Oh God, I love you and I thank you for your joy and peace. I thank you for your Holy Spirit that guides my every step. He said: *MY DAUGHTER IF YOU REMAIN IN SYNC WITH ME, YOU WILL NEVER WONDER WHAT YOUR NEXT MOVE WILL BE. YOU WILL DANCE WITH ME; YOU WILL MOVE WITH ME; MY THOUGHTS AND WAYS WILL BE REVEALED TO YOU AND YOU SHALL WALK ON WATER. I LOVE YOU, MY CHILD!*

Vision #3 (11:27 a.m.): As I lay on the threshing floor speaking in tongues, I saw myself as this beautiful woman running. Then I stopped, extended my hands and as I declared God's commands (in my spiritual language), I saw power flowing from my fingertips, everywhere I extended my hands, it flowed covering the entire scene. I spoke power, I spoke healing, I twirled around in a waltz-like circle in order to reach everything in sight. I don't know what was being said but I felt God's mercy surrounding me as power continued to be poured out. I twirled around in my long flowing dress as if I were still dancing with the Father! (**Acts 4:30, 31, 2 Timothy 1:7**).

Conclusion: I never thought that sowing seed, giving, and being obedient would lead to such discipline, blessings, and FREEDOM! I cannot express how liberated I feel, not being a hostage to "spending"! I have more money than I thought to give clearly not as much as credit affords, but I am at peace and I am still able to pay bills and occasionally splurge on some things I may want. The biggest blessing is when I presented my credit card to my husband for Valentine's Day with a pair of scissors (WHEW). I now have peace that passes all understanding; I have received that increment in my salary, I have confessed to my husband about my debt, and I am accountable to him with my spending habits. It feels so good not to be creating more debt and to be able to ask my husband for help which puts the power back into his hands as the provider. Most importantly to have a clear conscience!

PC: So how does it feel not to use the credit cards?

My Response: I feel so helpless and free all at the same time.

PC: The helplessness is just a feeling but FREEDOM is a Fact!

Next Level—Beyond The Veil!

Prayer (6:27 a.m.): As I closed my eyes and prayed, "God, I thank you for releasing me from the yoke of bondage; I thank you for canceling my debt. God, I give it all over to you and I ask you for help, guidance, mercy, grace, and favor. Lord, I ask you to cancel this debt so that I may be able to freely give and be a blessing to those in need. And so that I am able to sow willingly and freely so that my barnyards can overflow! I love you, Daddy, and I thank you for the ability to obtain wealth.

Vision: As I was praying, I was standing in front of a large curtain and I said, "God, I'm opening this curtain and removing the veil that I may stand before you in all of your glory!" As I pulled the curtain down, the light was extremely bright; I fell to my knees and began worshiping Him!!! I said, "Lord, I am ready to go to the next level. I no longer fear to take this step! Here I am, Lord, at your feet to do your will!!! The vision ended! I praised all the way to work excitedly saying "I'M BEYOND THE VEIL, LORD!!!!! I just kept repeating it because I have been in front of it several times and NEVER moved the curtain. I couldn't believe I was finally in this place!!! I declared: EVERYTHING I SPEAK FROM THIS DAY FORWARD WILL COME TO PASS WITH POWER AND AUTHORITY IN JESUS' NAME!!!!"

God's Response: *MY DEAREST, DAUGHTER, I AM SO PROUD OF YOU. CONTINUE TO MOVE FORWARD, CONTINUE TO LEARN OF ME, STAY AT MY FEET! NO MAN IS AN ISLAND AND NO ONE CAN FIX THIS BETTER THAN ME! I WILL HELP YOU IF YOU ASK ME! THE SEASON OF CANCELED DEBT IS UPON YOU! I CREATED THIS SEASON AND I CAN PERFORM IT! ASK AND YOU SHALL RECEIVE, SEEK AND KNOCK. I WILL WITHHOLD NOTHING FROM YOU IF YOU ASK!* (**Deuteronomy 15:1-6**)

PC: I'm Proud of You!! Now you can experience a Life of FREEDOM!! OK, Now, as you continue to talk to Victor, share with him how God laid Conviction in your Heart. This will allow him to see your Relationship with God differently and begin to make his own Relationship with God stronger because he'll see A GOD OF ORDER!!! Now, Diane, DON'T GO BACK FOR ANYTHING!! Because if you ever do, you may not be able to regain your Momentum Again! It's been a drilling few months but look at what God has done in just a short period of time, and now that the King and Queen are on the same page, the Princes and Princesses will fall in line with the Plan, God has for your Family's Kingdom!!!

Chapter VI: Relationship(s): I AM!

In order to get to the meat of this chapter, I have to first give a synopsis of my relationship(s). This chapter will be one of the many lessons I cover in this book and this will probably be my longest chapter because it involves Diane—the woman, wife, mother, and friend! These are the studies I was instructed to do, the Lessons I learned and my conversations with God and with PC!

Synopsis: "Relation" is the condition or state of one (entity/individual) in connection with another. "Ship" is a type of suffix; a word that is attached to the end of a base or root word to change its dynamics/meaning, or to express the quality, condition, or state of being. When you look at the word relationship, it doesn't matter which prefix is used: Kinship, partnership/marriage, or friendship, they all should have a common denominator: LOVE! In this chapter, I am exploring and dealing with the changes needed in me to enhance the dynamic of my love for God, family, my husband, my friends, life, and strangers…

I AM DAVID!

I was Instructed to study Matthew 7 but God also had me studying the Character of David.

Study (6:12 a.m.): David's Characteristic, *David owned his faults*: **2 Samuel 12:1-20**—In this chapter, a parable was given to David. It involved a scenario of the very thing he had done to someone else! He was furious and declared the punishment for the person who did wrong!!! Not even realizing he was condemning himself, lol. When it was revealed, he didn't deny that it happened and he didn't blame others. He said, "I have sinned against the Lord" and God punished him by killing the son born as a result of the sin committed. David accepted it, worshiped God and moved on! In David's day, this is how God handled sin today (**1 John 1:9, 10**). 9 *If we confess our sins, He is faithful and just to forgive us our sins and to cleanse us from all unrighteousness. 10 If we say that we have not sinned, we make Him a liar, and His word is not in us.* As I concluded this lesson, I confessed to God any sin, residue, things, he already knew that I had not let go of. This was His response:

MY PRECIOUS, DAUGHTER, CONFESSING SIN IS NOT SO THAT I CAN PUNISH YOU; CONFESSING SIN IS HEALING, CONFESSING SIN IS CLEANSING, CONFESSING SIN REMOVES IT FROM YOUR LIFE! THERE IS ALWAYS A RESIDUE OF SIN LEFT BEHIND WHEN YOU DON'T ACKNOWLEDGE IT AND ATTEMPT TO KEEP IT HIDDEN. ALWAYS REMEMBER I KNOW ABOUT IT, SO WHY HIDE IT? THESE ARE THE THINGS THAT KEEP YOU HUMBLE. WHEN YOU CAN ADMIT YOU ARE WRONG, IT KEEPS YOU FROM CONDEMNING OTHERS. I FORGIVE YOU! IT IS DONE! IT IS FORGOTTEN, NOW LET IT GO AND MOVE ON!

Confession: There are some things in my life that I'm not proud of and although my lifestyle has changed and I am no longer my old self, and I am no longer living out my old ways, I just moved on from it and I ALWAYS used to think about it off and on with shame and condemnation. Finally admitting it to God and hearing him tell me it is done, forgotten, and that I should move on, HAS TRULY FREED ME!!!! (**Romans 8:1**). Hallelujah!!! Thank you, God! This helps me understand

Matthew 7:1-5 even more. If God forgave my sins, who am I to condemn and judge someone else about something they did or are doing, especially if they've confided in me in order to get the help they need!!! Why would I continue to hold it over their head? I learned to PRAY, keep it moving, and not look back!!! *Love is NOT judgmental!

I AM UN-BOTHERED!

The other night I had been battling with a lying spirit and my integrity and character was being attacked. I wrestled with the things that were said about me all night long! Defending my honor in my sleep, tossing and turning. I woke up with it still on my mind.

Morning Study: *"Do not give dogs what is sacred; do not throw your pearls to pigs. If you do, they may trample them under their feet and turn and tear you to pieces* (**Matthew 7:6**).

I asked the Lord: What are MY pearls? His reply: your goodness, your truth, **your peace**!

This is what the Lord said to me: *DO NOT ATTEMPT TO DEFEND YOURSELF WITH TRUTH AGAINST THE TRICKS OF THE FATHER OF LIES! NOTHING YOU SAY WILL*

SATISFY A LYING SPIRIT. ITS JOB IS TO MAKE YOU APPEAR DECEITFUL! AND EVEN A FOOL IS THOUGHT WISE IF HE KEEPS SILENT AND DISCERNING IF HE HOLDS HIS TONGUE. REMAINING SILENT SIMPLY ALLOWS ONE TO AVOID THE FATE OF BEING THOUGHT A FOOL! HOLD YOUR PEACE WHICH IS YOUR PEARL! IF YOU CAST YOUR PEARLS TO PIGS, A LYING TONGUE WILL TRAMPLE OVER YOU: TALK OVER YOU, BULLY YOU, LIE, AND PROVE THEMSELVES TO BE RIGHT BY TAKING YOU OUT OF YOUR CHARACTER; DON'T DO IT! VENGEANCE IS MINE SAITH THE LORD. *Love is Peaceful!*

Proverbs 17:28 after that I held my peace and thought no more about it!

I AM CONVICTED!

On Monday morning, Study **Psalm 9:1**. David's characteristics; *David acknowledged God.* God took me to **Proverbs 3:5-6**. *Trust in the Lord with all your heart, and lean not on your own understanding; In all your ways acknowledge Him, And He shall direct your paths.*

Question Posed: What are the "ways" in which I can acknowledge God?

Lesson Learned (6:11 a.m.): As I was getting dressed this morning in the dark to avoid waking my husband up, he yelled out, "You can turn on the light, I'm already up." I said, "No, I'm good. I don't want you to get up early because then I have to rush to do for you which cuts into my time." He said, "I have to go change a tire anyway," so I conceded and said, "OK BUT I was not happy about it because I woke up a little late!" So I went upstairs to start my study and stopped at this question in order to fix my husband's breakfast. (What are the "ways" in which I can acknowledge God?) Still a little perturbed as I cooked, God gently said to me: *IN ALL YOUR WAYS ACKNOWLEDGE ME. WHY CAN'T YOU ACKNOWLEDGE ME WHEN SERVING YOUR HUSBAND?* My attitude toward what I was doing QUICKLY changed!!!

Prayer: Thank you, God, for correction, direction, and lessons! I love you! God then said: *MY DAUGHTER I PROMISED TO NEVER LEAVE YOU WITHOUT AN ANSWER OR A*

SOLUTION! I AM GLAD YOU ARE ABLE TO LISTEN, LEARN, AND OBEY! KEEP GOING!

Lesson Learned: It never dawned on me that serving my husband was an act of serving and acknowledging God! **(Colossians 3:18)**

PC: IN ALL THY WAYS, there is nothing you should be doing in which God is not being acknowledged; if there is then you shouldn't be doing it! Acknowledging Him always begins with your Attitude! Our thoughts are what get us into trouble because as we think so do we react! **(Proverbs 23:7)**. But when you approach everything as unto the Lord, your actions become different and you react differently. Stubbornness, attitudes, unwillingness, all begin to disappear! Which then creates different outcomes. Now that you've gotten this it opens another Door to another Level!! On this Level, you are Focusing on Creating an Attitude and a Mindset of God!! This is very important but it's also very difficult because you begin to lose more of your Will and Ways and begin to Take On the Will and Ways of God's Diane! This is when the scripture that says that the Flesh is against the Spirit and the Spirit against the

55

Flesh begins to make more sense (**Galatians 5:17**)! The Flesh Diane has been doing her thing most of your Life and now the Spirit Diane is bucking to be the Primary! It's a war that takes place between your Mind and Spirit. The More You Feed the Spirit, the Stronger You Become as A Whole!! This is going to Change how you See and Respond to EVERYTHING! Including how you deal with your husband. *Love SERVES!

I AM DELILAH!

I was instructed by PC to study the Characteristics of Delilah and see what God reveals to me about myself.

Delilah Study: **Judges 16**, *4 Sometime later, he fell in love with a woman in the Valley of Sorek whose name was Delilah 5 The rulers of the Philistines went to her and said, "See if you can lure him into showing you the secret of his great strength and how we can overpower him so we may tle him up and subdue him. Each one of us will give you eleven hundred shekels of silver…"*(So Delilah began her plot) *15 Then she said to him, "How can you say, 'I love you' when you won't confide in me? This is the third time you have made a fool of me and haven't told me the secret of your great strength." 16*

With such nagging she prodded him day after day until he was sick to death of it. 17 So he told her everything. "No razor has ever been used on my head," he said, "because I have been a Nazi-rite dedicated to God from my mother's womb. If my head were shaved, my strength would leave me, and I would become as weak as any other man." 18 When Delilah saw that he had told her everything, she sent word to the rulers of the Philistines, "Come back once more; he has told me everything." So the rulers of the Philistines returned with the silver in their hands. 19 After putting him to sleep on her lap, she called for someone to shave off the seven braids of his hair, and so began to subdue him. And his strength left him.

6:00 a.m.: A woman has the power to bring the strongest of men down to their knees, with or without even knowing it!

-The innocence in not knowing the power we hold can be dangerous to a man. This is why it is so important for us women to learn the strength of a man and the wisdom of how to help him grow into it!

-The world represents the Rulers of Palestine in a way that a black man fights daily against a cruel society that knows his strength and systematically plots and plans of ways to tear him down! This is where we "Delilahs" come in because they KNOW if they can break the family down, they can tear the foundation up!

Lesson: I am learning daily how to not use my powers (knowing my husband's vulnerabilities) for evil but good. I am learning how to support him in his business, and how to become his partner, not his problem. I am learning how to encourage him, how to build him up, and how to love him all the more so that his strength becomes OUR strength and his fight becomes our fight! This is absolutely not easy because as we see from the story a man will not come out and be completely honest about his struggles. So patience is needed, discernment is needed, understanding is needed, and LOVE is needed.

Question: What in Delilah do I see about my self TODAY?

- The frustration of not knowing what's going on with my husband at times.

Question: What has this taught me?

- At times I have to be my husband's strength; he will grow weary and frustrated (and I may not know and may not need to know why) but I still have to use my influence to encourage him!

Prayer: God, help me to be my husband's strength in his time of weakness. Give me the wisdom to encourage him and not cause him harm. We are ONE so if he is weak so am I, but in YOU we are made strong! Help me to always uplift him with this good news! You are our strength, our joy, our love, our power, and our God!!! I love you, Lord!

God said: *MY PRECIOUS GEM; I LOVE YOU AND I AM SO PROUD OF THE WOMAN AND WIFE YOU ARE BECOMING! CONTINUE TO SEEK MY FACE AND YOU WILL NOT FAIL AT ANYTHING YOU PUT YOUR HANDS TO. YOUR HUSBAND IS BLESSED! HE IS A REFLECTION OF ME AND A PRIZE TO YOU! I AM HIS STRENGTH! BY GRACE YOU ARE HIS POWER. HOW YOU LOVE HIM WILL CONTINUE TO BE HIS SOURCE; THAT LOVE IS MY LOVE THAT I HAVE GIVEN YOU FOR HIM. DO NOT STRAY OR SWAY FROM THAT LOVE; HE NEEDS IT AND*

ULTIMATELY YOU NEED IT! LOVE IS YOUR STRENGTH!!!

SELAH!

PC's Response: Now this is AWESOME!!! YOU GOT IT!!! Well, this makes me Proud you have Matured to a Level that God Revealed to you the Secret or Source of the Marriage Strength! There should Never be any more Doubt about what your part in the Marriage is! So if you slack off in the Love department, you Weaken your Husband!! This is a Lesson that will Empower Women/Wives EVERYWHERE!!

My Response: YES! And after I finished my lesson and was about to leave the house, I ran downstairs and kissed and kissed and kissed (mwah) my husband's face, lol, and told him, "I LOVE YOU!" This truly has empowered me with understanding and it encourages me to keep doing what I am doing!

PC's Response: Yes, you have the right to be Excited today; another Level Accomplished! Have you noticed that every time you go Up, your Marriage grows Closer! Now when you see your husband getting into Worship at the church that's going to be another Confirmation! God is slowly reeling him in; you see as a fisherman you reel in the Big fish differently lol you can't rush, and you have to be mindful of how much Tension you apply as you Patiently reel them in! God is reeling your husband in Patiently and Carefully!! Soon when people say, "They're a Wealthy Family," it'll be in every area of your Lives!! It's easier for you to Love your husband now that you Completely understand what your Love is and what it does!!

*Love is Strength! **Proverbs 31:10-12**

I AM ESTHER!

My study this morning consists of "Greener Grass."

Esther 1, concentrating on verse 5, 8 & 9 *When these days were over, the king gave a banquet, lasting seven days, in the enclosed garden of the king's palace, for all the people from the least to the greatest who were in the citadel of Susa. By the king's command each guest was allowed to drink with no restrictions, for the king instructed all the wine stewards to serve each man what he wished. Queen Vashti also gave a banquet for the women in the royal palace of King Xerxes.*

Men vs Women at the "banquet"

What is the difference between a gathering of men versus women? **Men:** Drink, have fun, unwind, relax, and let go; they do things they cannot do at home. **Women:** Become empowered, vent or boast, build each other up, and become enlighten and encouraged by something someone else is doing!

Women: When we get together, someone is bound to be speaking excitedly about how good their relationship is. **Men:** Men don't typically come out the gate bragging on their wives/woman they ease into it saying little things here and there. They are more protective, not trying to cause other men to covet their wives, especially if they are dropping the ball in certain areas. **Women:** We come to the table ready to prove how wonderful our relationship is and how "perfectly" we are being treated. We find validation in being able to say we are with a man who treats us right. **Question:** So what happens when the party's over? For a woman who may not be receiving as much as the other women but has a good man? She goes home ARMED! Lol. We are now putting stipulations on what was a decent relationship and our man doesn't have a clue what's going on!

*I can definitely relate to this when I see flowers being delivered to my job for a co-worker from their husband. This doesn't necessarily mean they have a better marriage but it opens the door for me to notice my lack or a desire which is not being met. It's like a child with an old beat-up toy; they love that toy and play with it every day! But cousin Tommy comes over with this shiny new toy that doesn't do as much but it's shiny!

Lesson: When I (we) see my sister happy and bragging on her man, I will celebrate with her!!! Not have the attitude that she is faking nor will I try to look for holes in her story. We don't know how she got where she is at, we don't know what God had to do in that relationship to get them where they are. And if she's been treated well from the door and this man came into her life and swept her off of her feet, we don't know how many men used and abused her prior to that relationship! The key is to Learn what needs to change in myself to create that kind of "bragging rights." How I can see the best in my relationship to lift my man up and create an environment that allows him to want to treat me like a queen and brag openly to his partners!

After doing this study, I was able to change the atmosphere in my home; I had still been "recovering" from a disagreement the other night so I was NOT myself and I knew my husband felt it (his tail was between his legs). But I went downstairs hugged him tightly, we kissed....... and I told him, "I love you, Babe." I felt a shift and saw the grass turning greener! *Love is Positive!

I AM WHO GOD SAYS I AM!

So God is working on me with my faith! (**James 1:2-8**). A lot of times we say "stretch" your faith but that would be relying on the strength we currently have; stretching weakens as does a rubber band when stretched; rubber bands are unpredictable and weaken eventually popping! God said, "He wants to STRENGTHEN my faith for endurance so that I can handle anything!"

Stretching is pulling something, forcing it to reach its "natural" capacity. Exercising is working the muscle to strengthen it so that you are capable of going beyond the natural into the supernatural!

My desire is to get to a place where I am not forced into doing anything or to where someone doesn't have to pull things out of me!

I was instructed by PC to write down on on paper who am I?

I wasn't really sure so I asked God: Who am I?

This is His reply: *MY SPECIAL GEM!

*COURAGEOUS—YOU'VE WON MANY BATTLES!

*FAITHFUL—YOU NEVER GIVE UP

*WISE—I HAVE POURED SO MUCH OF MY WISDOM INTO YOU; YOU ARE EMPOWERED!

*FEARLESS—FEAR DOESN'T OWN YOU ANYMORE, YOU'VE BEEN RELEASED!

*ANOINTED— I HAVE GIVEN YOU MANY GIFTS, SOME YOU HAVE NOT SEEN AS OF YET

*FUNNY—YES, EVEN I LAUGH AT YOUR JOKES!

*BOLD—YOU HAVE GROWN SO MUCH IN THIS AREA!

*PASSIONATE—YOU HAVE A VERY KIND AND GIVING HEART

*WORSHIPER—YOUR LOVE FOR ME IS EVIDENT!

God asked me: SO *WHO DO YOU SAY THAT I AM?* My reply to Him: My Daddy, my God, My Lord, the lover of my soul, my best friend, my help, my savior, my redeemer, my joy, my strength, you are my healer, my deliver, my solution, my power, you are my calm, my peace, you are my EVERYTHING!!!

Then He asked: *WHAT DO YOU KNOW YOU CAN DO THROUGH ME?*

*all things!!!

*cast out demons, trample over serpents

*call into existence those things that are not

*heal, deliver, set captives free!

*sing, make people smile and laugh

*fight! have self-control, forgive

*pray

*encourage

*be decisive and assertive!

God: *THIS LIST IS THE ESSENCE OF WHO YOU ARE*!

Lesson I Learned: IF I truly believe what I wrote then the trials that come into my life do not and will not have the capability to break me but everything I endure will strengthen my faith in God and believe him to be exactly what I say He is to me and most importantly to trust in who He says I AM! *Love is not stretched it is strengthened!

I AM HIGHER!

Vision 7:15 p.m.: I had a vision of Large hands reaching out to me from the sky. As I stood in my room with my eyes closed and my heart open I begin to weep! I lifted my hands up in the air to touch the Large hands reaching down to me. I heard the Lord saying *"COME UP HIGHER"*! I replied, "Yes, Daddy!" As I said this, the sky got dark with thick thunderous clouds to where I could not see his hands. I heard the Lord saying, *"DO YOU STILL WANT TO COME UP HIGHER?"* I waved my hands as to clear the sky and I screamed out "PEACE! BE STILL." The clouds disappeared, I began stretching my hands up to grab the Lord's hands as he pulled me up! I looked down and I could see vibrant, colorful flowers everywhere! All kinds of animals looking up praising the Master. Upon seeing this in the spirit, while in my room with my eyes closed I fell to my knees and I cried uncontrollably!!! I KNEW I was in the presence of the Almighty God! *Love desires to go higher!

I AM A MOTHER!

My study this morning was in **Genesis 21 concentrated verses 17-19** 17. *God heard the boy crying, and the angel of God called to Hagar from heaven and said to her, "What is the matter, Hagar? Do not be afraid; God has heard the boy crying as he lies there. 18 Lift the boy up and take him by the hand, for I will make him into a great nation." 19* **Then _God opened her eyes and she saw a well of water._** *So she went and filled the skin with water and gave the boy a drink.* **What I learned:** As a mother, it's hard to detach from the pain of our children (regardless of their age). When they get hurt we get hurt! But our despair can blind us from seeing God's comfort and help! In our worry, concern, and helplessness, we become so consumed by burdens that we don't see the remedy God has already provided right in front of our eyes. My comforting scripture in dealing with my children is: Start children off on the way they should go, and even when they are old they will not turn from it (**Proverbs 22:6**).

Genesis 21, 15 *And the water in the skin was used up, and she placed the boy under one of the shrubs. 16 Then she went and sat down across from him at a distance of about a bow shot; for she said to herself, "Let me not see the death of the boy." So she sat opposite him, and lifted her voice and wept. 17* **And God heard the voice of the lad.**

What I also learned is: There comes a time when God no longer goes through the parent but will deal directly with the child! This is especially true in the case of adult children who have to develop their own relationship with God as we did. This has been an extremely hard lesson, to pray and still watch your children make a poor decision and/or to have no control over their path. My comforting scripture is **Proverbs 3:5, 6** I am learning daily how to trust the process and the promises God made regarding my offspring! And besides the problem will not go away just because we hide from it!

As I cried out to God regarding a pressing issue I knew my adult son was struggling with this is what the Lord said to me. **(6:45 a.m.):** *MY DAUGHTER, I AM WITH YOU ALWAYS. I HEAR YOUR CRIES AND THE CRIES OF YOUR CHILDREN.*

I WILL HELP THEM; I WILL MAKE GREATNESS POUR OUT OF YOUR LINEAGE. I HAVE NOT FORGOTTEN YOU, MY DAUGHTER; FEAR NOT FOR I HEAR THE CRIES OF YOUR CHILDREN! I WILL HEAL YOUR LAND! (Psalm 112:1, 2). *Love is Maternal!

I AM ONE!

So today was my first experience of spiritual "ONENESS" with my husband. After Prayer and Study, I had to drive my husband to work this morning because my stepson sporadically went to Florida and my husband was feeling some kind of way about it. He is NOT a morning person, so on the way to his job he was nitpicking. We got in the car and my mirrors had rain on them but I could see out of them. He suggested I clean them off but I felt I didn't need to, so I didn't wipe them off; I began to go on the HWY and I stated, "I can't see the traffic merging." He said with an undertone, "That's why you should have cleaned the mirror off!" I started to say something but I stopped myself; he then said, "See I'm right that's why you can't say anything." So I said, "No, actually I couldn't see out of the mirror because our daughter changed my view when she drove the other day," and he went, "OH." I could tell something was OFF with him and wondered if our son's going to Florida had something to do with it! Then he began to aggressively question me about our daughter regarding her decision to go to the National Guard, college, etc. I politely told him I already handled it but I will double-check the paperwork to make sure everything she needs is provided and we are well prepared. I was quiet for the rest of the ride! As he got out of the car, I kissed him goodbye, wished him well, and drove to work. But I felt like someone was sitting on my shoulders; a heaviness!

As I was driving to work, I said to the Lord, "This was NOT how I thought my morning would go. I got up, prayed, did my study, and worshiped. "I" was in a WONDERFUL mood, feeling great until this drive! God said to me, *"WHAT YOU ARE FEELING IS HOW YOUR HUSBAND FEELS THIS MORNING; YOU ARE ONE! SO WHAT ARE YOU GOING TO DO ABOUT IT?!"* I began to pray for him asking God to relieve and release him for all anxiety. I could barely breathe due to the heaviness; the more I prayed the heavier it got, I began to blow into the atmosphere to clear away the "fog"; I went in calling out and casting out anything that came into my spirit! I blessed him and lifted him up as I was praying. I could literally feel the weight lifting off of my shoulders and a light crisp breeze of freshness in my car to where I could breathe easy. I just started praising God for lifting him up! I was completely fine after that. I sent my husband an "I love you" text with a blessing and called him around 1:30 p.m. He sounded SO MUCH BETTER!!!

Lesson Learned: In the past, I wouldn't have understood what was happening and would have been ALL in my feelings today. I learned we are one. BUT GOD!!!! (**Genesis 2:24**). *Love is Patient!

I AM DEBT FREE!

Lesson: *A good person leaves an inheritance for his/her children's children, but a sinner's wealth is stored up for the righteous* (**Proverbs 13:22**). *God knew my heart's desire and concern. (I do not want to leave behind debt; I want to leave an inheritance!)

Transparency: Since committing to getting out of debt my bank account has shrunk to nearly nothing because I am no longer using credit to subsidize my needs/wants. This has been challenging for me and a little scary. Credit cards are not bad when used properly; however, at the time of my use, I was not educated on how to keep my balances low and pay off what I spend. So I am so far out of balance that the only thing I can do is make double payments until I receive my breakthrough.

Prayer: Daddy, I love you and I want to do your will. Please forgive me for the path I have taken in my finances. Lord, please help me to correct my error! I need you, Lord, open up the flood gates and pour out a blessing. I declare this day that I AM DEBT FREE!!!!

God's Response: *OBEDIENCE IS BETTER THAN SACRIFICE. I DO NOT WISH FOR YOU TO SACRIFICE YOUR FINANCES, HEALTH, NOR DO I INTEND ON BRINGING YOU TO POVERTY. YOU ARE RICH IN ME, ALL OF THE WEALTH OF THIS LAND BELONGS TO ME! YOU CANNOT LOOK TO CHANCE, LUCK, OR LOTTO. I AM THE WAY OF LIFE, I AM THE WAY TO WEALTH. FOLLOW*

ME, FOLLOW MY INSTRUCTIONS AND YOU WILL BE OK. YOU WILL LIVE IN ABUNDANCE. YOU WILL BE A LENDER AND NOT A BORROWER. I WILL MAKE THE CROOKED PATH STRAIGHT! TRUST ME, DIANE! (This is the first time in a long time he used my name.)

PC's Response: This was GOOD!!! Your lessons/prayers are becoming More Intense! More strategic, More Direct! Your Relationship with God has grown. When God uses the terms Daughter, Child, etc., He's speaking to you on that level but when He addresses you by name, it's because you have Matured in Him and He now speaks to you as a Spiritually Mature Adult! Now periodically He may still use these terms of endearment but He still sees you as a Matured Daughter! Which also means He Expects MORE! *When I was a Child I did Childish things, but when I became an Adult I put away Childish Things!* (**1 Corinthians 13:11**). He Expects More. He's going to Expect you to react with the response of a Mature Daughter! Which means you're going to have to Step It Up with Your TRUST. *Love is Maturing!

I AM CLOSER!

Last night before going to Choir rehearsal, I felt the urge to just spend time in God's presence. I took my oil out, anointed my head (mind), lips (speech), my ears (to hear clearly), my hands (to let go and to receive), and my feet (to move with fire and to walk as directed). As I worshiped, God just filled me with his presence and I could no longer do anything but drop to my knees and wail! I could feel his touch on me and I just cried out "God, I love you, I need you, I want you. I had an overwhelming urgency and desire just to be close to him. It was a wonderful experience! (**James 4:8**).

PC's Response: This Process is going to appear to be strenuous at times. You're going to be instructed to move when you can't see how or where. You're going to be instructed to give your last, and sometimes give what you don't see. Speak when you're normally quiet. You've asked to be Closer. Well, being Closer comes with a price, and the price is to Move in Complete Obedience, Boldness, and Faithfulness!

My response: WHEW! Oh Great, Diane, look what you got us into now! (Me speaking to myself in the third person.)

PC: Yep you wanted it lol, and it appears that God took you up on it! There's no more room or time to be asking How and Why, now it's just OK Done!! The flip side to this is you're in a Great Position to Speak what you want, if you can get to the Complete Trust factor you'll be Living in Complete Abundance!! You now have to Condition yourself to SPEAK, EXPECT, RECEIVE! Because God is Expecting you to HEAR, COMPLY, AND DO…

My Response: Wow! I cannot wait to see "Diane" doing this... I am in AWE of the thought! I've often moved by faith but it was limited; now to supersede that is going to be exciting!!! This will be the realm of Prophetic Manifestations! (Me speaking to myself in 3rd person again lol.)*Love grows closer!

I AM SPIRITUAL!

This morning I was tapping into getting to know the Holy Spirit!

1 Corinthians 2: 10 these are the things God has revealed to us by his Spirit. The Spirit searches all things, even the deep things of God. 11 For who knows a person's thoughts except their own spirit within them? In the same way no one knows the thoughts of God except the Spirit of God.

Study: You must DWELL not visit (Consistency)...

He who DWELLS in the secret place of the Most High God will abide (live, remain, stay, continue with). To me this means no more "playing" church! And no more drive-by prayers (**Psalms 91:1**).

Confession: In examining myself I can honestly say 80 percent of my prayer life is "fleshly," meaning I believed that the more "emotional" I got when praying meant the more "spiritual" or in the spirit I was, so once I finished "snotting," I was done and I got up. How much energy I wasted on empty vague praying that produced NO power! (**Matthew 6:7**). God desires for me to DWELL. Be Still, stay put and in some cases, BE QUIET! My encounter the other day during prayer is exactly what God desires from me ALWAYS; not just a laundry list of wants, needs, and cares, he already knows all about them. But there are things he wants ME to know about Him and about his plan for me that ONLY the spirit can teach me! BE STILL AND KNOW.

*Emotions are not spiritual however emotions can be produced from a SPIRITUAL encounter.

Encounter: This morning while using the restroom I was playing Donald Lawrence's song "Let me be Spiritual." As I was singing, God interrupted my session, lol, I said, "Really God, while I'm on the toilet"? He said, "YES!" I chuckled. This is what he said to me (**7:43 a.m.**): *SPIRITUAL YOU DESIRE; SPIRITUAL I WILL GIVE YOU BUT YOU MUST PROTECT THE DEPOSIT!!! NO MORE FRIVOLOUS BEHAVIOR, ACTS, THOUGHTS, PRAYERS, AND/OR DESIRES. YOU MUST THINK SPIRITUAL, WALK SPIRITUAL, TALK SPIRITUAL, LIVE SPIRITUAL. MY HOLY SPIRIT WILL TEACH YOU WHAT YOU NEED TO KNOW; JUST WALK IN IT! BE STILL AND KNOW THAT I AM GOD!* (**Psalm 46:10**)

Encounter #2: So I'm in the kitchen fixing my breakfast. I like drinking a cup of coffee in the morning. I don't use sugar but I drown it with cream (for sweetness). I clearly heard the Holy Spirit say, *"CHANGE YOUR EATING HABITS!"* I was like OK (thinking to myself, MAN God is all up in my mix this morning! lol). I've been eating somewhat healthy but God was showing me another level of discipline; he showed me John when he was in the wilderness eating locust and honey (**Matthew 3:4**). NOT THAT I AM SUPPOSED TO EAT THAT, lol, but the strength and stamina he possessed. *The Holy Spirit just showed me as I was typing this: NO BREAD AND NO WINE. Jesus get me through this! (**Luke 7:33**). **How effective can God's people be if we are always sick, bogged down, unhealthy, can't move, can't breathe, can't focus, popping pills, and unable to travel! *Love is Healthy!

I AM SPIRIT!

God told me today that I cannot grasp the fullness of his hidden wisdom until I truly know His spirit in me!

I am excited about this adventure and learning this lesson but most excited about the results and the POWER that is coming from it.

Study: But you will receive power when the Holy Spirit comes on you and you will be my witnesses in Jerusalem, and in all Judea and Samaria, and to the ends of the earth (**Acts 1:8**).

*There are no "God" results in the flesh, only in the Spirit!

(**Galatians 5:16-18**)

The first step to disarming the flesh is to empower your spirit!

(**Romans 8:13**). *For if you live according to the flesh, you will die; but if by the Spirit, you put to death the misdeeds of the body; you will live.*

How to disarm the flesh? FEED THE SPIRIT with God's word!

-change eating habits: **Proverbs 23:21**

-change how I speak: **Colossians 4:6**

-change what I speak about: **Proverbs 18:21**

-transform my thinking: **Philippians 4:8**

-change what I watch: **Matthew 6:22, 23**

-change how I react: **Philippians 4:6, 7**

These are obvious to me but not easy because they are obvious! The spirit was given to ALL who believe but the manifestation of the spirit is discovered by few! God said to me: *THIS IS THE HIDDEN WISDOM I DESIRE YOU TO POSSESS... MANIFESTATION!* Paul said in **1 Corinthians 2:4-5** *My message and my preaching were not with wise and persuasive words, but with a demonstration of the Spirit's power, so that* *your faith might not rest on human wisdom, but on God's power.*

Manifestation allows us to see the unseen, to do the impossible! This Gift is given to any and all **1 Corinthians 12** 7 *But the manifestation of the Spirit is given to every man to profit withal.* But rarely do we SEE the demonstration of the gifting because we utilize them in the FLESH! (doubt, conceit, fear, operating in our own strength, and lack of faith) This is seen in **Matthew 17:14-21** when the disciples could not cast out a demon. Verse *19 Then the disciples came to Jesus in private and asked, "Why couldn't we drive it out?" 20 He replied, "Because you have so little faith. Truly I tell you, if you have faith as small as a mustard seed, you can say to this mountain, 'Move from here to there', and it will move. Nothing will be impossible for you."* The unfortunate part in all of this is FEW are chosen (**Matthew 22:14**) and most of those that are chosen haven't paid attention to "the call"! God has been calling us OUT into the deep, calling us to walk on water, to trust, to move mountains, but most of us don't even believe in this kind of power/manifestations! We are happy with "dancing," happy with "feeling the spirit," happy with "the duty" of the church but not the "deity" of God's divine POWER! Thus, people walk in and out of the building getting equipped but having no idea what to do with the tools they receive. This is where the Prophetic guidance comes into play. Just as Eli helped Samuel identify with God's Rhema calling, **1 Samuel 3** Prophets help take the tools we learn in the building and apply them to the spiritual gifts God reveals to them that are in us! The Prophet of God guides us through the visions we see, helps us understand the Rhema words we hear, and assists us with identifying the specific instructions given by the Holy Spirit — through their leading we end up doing something extra ordinary, blessing others, bless our own lives and ultimately bringing glory to God! We must die to self and flesh; get over the skepticism and walk by faith! Be open and readily available for God to have His way in us, through us, and with us! We must believe that God can do exactly what he says he can do!

Prayer: God, I thank you for your wisdom in learning about the Spirit at work in me. I thank you that this is the first step in walking in the manifestation of your gifting(s) that I have! I love you, Daddy, and I want to do your will. Thank you for removing the distractions and the skepticism so that I can have this time solely for getting all that you desire for me to have from your teachings.

God said: *MY LOVING DAUGHTER, YOU ARE THE APPLE OF MY EYE AND I CHERISH YOU! YOU ARE QUICKLY LEARNING THE SIMPLE. THIS WILL CATAPULT YOU TO THE DEEP. CONTINUE TO HEAR MY SPIRIT DIRECTING YOU AND DO ALL THAT IT REVEALS EVEN WHEN YOUR MIND TELLS YOU IT IS MINUTE! EVEN IN THOSE AREAS, I AM WORKING SOME THINGS OUT IN YOU! IT IS ALL FOR MY PURPOSE AND MY GLORY, BUT YOU WILL BENEFIT MIGHTILY FROM IT ALL. IT ALL HAS A DIVINE PURPOSE! *Love is Manifested!

I AM HAVING A MOMENT!

3:24 a.m.: I saw a vision of a hand knocking feverishly at a door. Research: A door represents an imaginary barrier through which a person passes when opened. Knocking on it means being almost ready to go through it. Knocking is a form of prayer! Ask, seek, knock (**Matthew 7:7**). I asked the Lord what He was trying to show me? This is what He said: *MY BEAUTIFUL DAUGHTER, YOU ARE ON YOUR WAY TO GLORY. THERE ARE SOME MINOR THINGS THAT STILL STAND IN YOUR WAY, THAT BLOCK YOUR PATH. KNOCK!!! PRAY TO RECEIVE WHATEVER YOU NEED TO GET TO THE OTHER SIDE AND I WILL OPEN THE DOOR TO YOU. PERSISTENCE! PRAY WITHOUT CEASING!*

(1Thessalonians 5:17)

Events: On Sunday, the spirit in the church was SUPER HIGH. I am enjoying being on the Praise Team. I enjoy evoking the power I KNOW I possess into the atmosphere. It's such a different feeling to operate in boldness and authority!!! The Sermon was on Taking Authority, walking in Boldness, and the power in prayer to do both! (so fitting) After church my family and I went out to eat; I had water due to a fast PC placed me on, but I was OK. Victor is doing EXACTLY what PC said he would do; I see him just staring, gazing lol and he is so much more passionate and attentive to me! I'm loving it! I, of course, continue to affirm him as I also see myself looking at him different; I've always loved him and appreciated him but God has taken it to a deeper level!

2:31 a.m.: I heard the Rhema words. *BE MINDFUL OF HOW YOU SPEAK AND WHAT YOU SAY!*

I prayed and asked God for clarity. This is what he said: *A DAY IS SOON TO COME WHERE POWER WILL FLOW FROM YOUR HEART TO YOUR MOUTH AND IT WILL BE MANIFESTED!!! I NEED YOU TO TRAIN YOUR MIND SO THAT OUT OF YOUR BOSOM FLOWS THE BREATH OF LIFE! YOU WILL HAVE POWER, ADAPT THE MIND OF CHRIST!* (**1 Corinthians 2:16**).

Events since I have been at work today: I found out the Board is voting on an increase in salaries for a select group of people due to equity issues. I am in that group! This is in addition to the end of the year increase I received. LOOK AT GOD! Now he is just showing off!!! GLORY! I don't know when this will be manifested but I CLAIM IT; IN THE NAME OF JESUS IT IS MINE!

PC: WOW!! This is what I call a GOD WEEKEND! You keep experiencing these Types of results because of your Obedience and willingness to Follow the Plan!! Have you noticed that each week your Testimony gets Stronger and it reaches outside of your home, and that's because you started in Order: You, Your Marriage, Your Family, Ministry, now the results are Manifesting in Order! You, Victor, Children, Home, Business, Church, and now Employment! While others are in fear because of the Shutdown, God is Opening Up Doors for You!

My Response: Yes, I see it!!! I had no clue how releasing some things, confessing some things, stepping up into some things, and giving, would take me to another level but I am not stopping because I know there is greater!!!

PC: YES, THERE IS GREATER!! Your prayers have been answered, your Seeds have just begun to sprout, and the growth in the business has yet to manifest (or has it?) And we are about to begin to Strengthen/Empower your Words with this next Study! The Growth of the Business is going to keep a Consistent flow of the Family's Finances for the Future and Growth doesn't always mean More, sometimes it's just Organizing and Tightening Up in certain areas! You haven't even begun to Witness the Favor that God has for you!! What you may not have realized is behind every Instruction that you Follow, Immediately God produces results, and every time you Increase your Seeds, God Increases your Finances! And this is just the beginning! Just imagine what will happen if you really took an Extreme Leap of Faith?

My Response: YES!!!!

PC: Now if we can get you to Leap without thinking and Analyzing What God places in your Heart and Spirit, it would quicken this Process! When God moves your Heart and Spirit, He expects you to Move Immediately not when you get a chance, not after you've thought about it, not after you've analyzed it, not after you've prayed over it but IMMEDIATELY! You don't have to pray about what HE SAYS, you don't need to Analyze it or Think about it because it's NOT GOING TO MAKE SENSE, and the Moment You Receive It that's when He Wants You To Move!!

My Response: You are absolutely correct and that is what he is working on with me right now, whew!!! I'm so complicated lol.

A part of my prayer that I didn't include was God help me to trust you and the places you tell me to go, the things you tell me to do, etc. put a fire under my feet so that I don't second guess you!

PC: Here's what I want you to do. Ask yourself a question that only you can answer. Why Don't I Completely Trust God? Now that may open up some areas in you that you haven't faced! There's a reason, and it could very well just be Fear of Failing or Falling!!

My Response: I can tell you one reason:

It's not God, it's the God in ME that I don't fully trust so I second guess what I hear just to make sure I "Diane" heard correctly and/or am following right. This stems from low self-esteem, feeling inadequate, remnants of abuse I assume. Yes, I am beginning to walk in boldness but I feel hesitant at times; there's still some timidity there!

There is no doubt in my mind that I am hearing God speak, seeing his visions, trusting the dreams and promises he's made to me but it's almost like I'm sitting on the sideline watching instead of seeing him using ME to do it (if this makes sense).

PC: Yes, it makes sense, and we need to move you pass your Fear of Getting in The Game! Because Yes He Wants to Use YOU! Why not you? Everyone He has ever used has been Broken, Hurt, Cast Aside, Overlooked, Beaten, Bruised, Whipped, Abused, Misused, and More!! Diane, you can do this!! Just look at what God has already Done!! See your Dreams come to Reality and Your Visions Being Manifested! See your Children where you know God Has Promised you to take them, see your Marriage at an All-Time High Every day, and then see your Ministry of Song taking you to places you never dreamed of!! Miracles after Miracles.

My Response: Something about this is hitting me hard! Because it is taking everything in me not to cry at work!!!

PC: God is trying to get you FREE! Go to the restroom and let it out!!! Let God do what He wants! He knows you're at work but He also knows it's TIME!

(Bathroom break....)

My Response: I've spent my entire life downplaying myself to make others feel comfortable in their own skin and at other times being put down, shut down, and let down just because of what the world deems as "beauty"! God said: *NO MORE!!!! IT'S NOT NEEDED; IT NEVER WAS!!!* I declared: I WILL WALK IN CONFIDENCE WITH BOLDNESS AND I WILL NOT COWER DOWN. I WILL WALK IN GRACE, SPEAK WITH GRACE, LEAD WITH GRACE, FOLLOW WITH GRACE, AND SING WITH GRACE IN JESUS' NAME. AMEN!!! *Love is Emotional!

I AM Deborah!

Lesson: Study Deborah the Wife! **Judges 4:4**: Now Deborah, a prophet, the wife of Lapidoth, was leading Israel at that time.

Deborah was Wise, Courageous, powerful, discerning, a Prophetess, and a Judge. Deborah's husband was unknown; his background was not talked about. Who he was or how he was but he was mentioned!

The name Lapidoth is Hebrew. It means TORCH, to enlighten, lamps! People with this name tend to be orderly and dedicated to building their lives on a solid foundation of order and service. They value truth, justice, and discipline, and maybe quick-tempered with those who do not. Their practical nature makes them good at managing and saving money, and at building things in the material world. Because of their focus on order and practicality, they may seem overly cautious and conservative at times. People with this name have a deep inner need for quiet, and a desire to understand and analyze the world they live in, and to learn the deeper truths.

When I read the personality of Deborah's husband's name, I couldn't help but notice some are identical to the character of my husband! Down to the tiniest detail! Although Deborah was a Judge, a Prophetess, and an important prominent person in the land of Israelites, God made it important to address her as the wife of Lapidoth in the scriptures. This tells me that no matter what path God has me on, I will always be connected to my husband; I will always be known as Victor's wife! He is my TORCH! He keeps me grounded! When I look at him, I see a greater purpose and something to fight for! He balances me and helps me learn daily! It is important for me to understand this because so many women who are in the service for God, who may have a more prominent path/position in the kingdom, tend to leave their husbands behind. I was definitely one of these women because I felt like my husband wasn't growing and I felt like he was holding me back. But Glory to God for correction and ORDER! I was holding myself back by being out of order! I am humbled by this revelation and grateful for the man I have in my life! This lesson gave me a deeper appreciation for my husband!!!!

Prayer: Thank you, God, for blessing me with a man after your own heart; a man of order, a man of faith, a man of discipline, and my anchor! When he found me I was a MESS! Thank you for using him to create peace for me and to teach me principles about money and wealth-building and the importance of leaving an inheritance. I thank you, God, because I am free to grow! I AM VICTOR'S WIFE "Diane," the prophetess, the judge, the mother, the life coach, the author, and your special gem! It's in Jesus' name I pray, Amen!

PC's Response: This Lesson allows you to see that just by God mentioning your name speaks Volumes! Yes, Victor stays in the Background but it's because of him that you are able to Glow!! He ignites your Flame!! See people often Focus on the ones out front and never think about what's holding them up, who ignites them, who pours into them, who refuels them.

Victor saw a Diamond in the rough, he saw his Assignment!! Had he not accepted his Assignment, where would you have been. It was in God's Divine Order for Victor to Plant God to Water, Nurture, and Prune God wants to increase you, so Victor could enjoy the Fruit of his Seeds!

My Response: This morning before I left the house (after I submitted my lesson), God told me to go downstairs and tell my husband what I was feeling.

I turned the light on so he could see my face; I needed him to know I meant what I was about to say. I said, "I love you! and I thank God for the blessing in you. I am so in Awe of you (he looked skeptic); I said you have taught me so much and I am learning from you. I may be moving slow but know that I am doing my very best and I will not stop until I become the woman and wife you desire for me to be." (My eyes began to water.) He KNEW I was sincere!

His face lit up like a cake with 100 candles on it!!! I hugged him again and told him I loved him so much He said "I love you too" I blessed his day with peace and I left to go to work!

PC's Response: You have a choice, stay where you are and be comfortable or Grow and be Happy, Radiant, and Prosperous.

My Response: I'll take the latter Alec for 200 (in my Jeopardy contestant voice)! "Who is" grow and be happy, radiant, and prosperous! Lol

PC's Response: You're really in Rare Form today. Victor gets you all perked up and I've got to deal with you (shaking my head lol). *Love is Humorous!

I AM GOMER!

I was instructed to study Hosea 1

Lesson: Hosea was sent to experience the very thing God condemned the people for and that he would later redeem them from. Why? Hosea's experience gave him an understanding and showed extreme obedience to God! Verse 2: *When the Lord began to speak through Hosea, the Lord said to him, "Go, marry a promiscuous woman and have children with her, for like an adulterous wife this land is guilty of unfaithfulness to the Lord." 3 So he married Gomer, daughter of Diblaim, and she conceived and bore him a son.* Hosea was to be the example for him to say, "Yes, I'm here with you doing the

94

same thing you are doing but I know someone who can help bring US out! (at that time to deal with a harlot/adulterous woman was punishable by death). But he was also used to bring redemption to the woman God had him choose. She was known to her town as a promiscuous woman yet God chose an "upper class" man to marry her!

*Testimony: I can remember prior to me and my husband's dating (after my separation and divorce from my first husband). Back then he was a Coach in the Athletic Ministry and I was a team mom (assistant to the Director of the Athletic Ministry at our church). So I did everything from cleaning toilets (straight from work) in heels to keeping score for each game. Everyone wondered about "me." Who is she? What's the deal with her? Is she married, single, etc.? But one thing that was obvious was I had four children who did not look alike... so the assumption was they must have different dads (which was correct!). There was "Water cooler" talk among the men (she must be easy) and "coffee conversation" among the insecure women (she's a harlot/hoe). These were "church folk" y'all, lol. In spite of all the "talk," God took the most successful and I believe the most handsome man among them all to choose to redeem ME. Most of the women wanted him (and some of them had him temporarily lol) and most of the men showed a secret desire towards me (of course, none would verbally admit it but the eyes and spirit tell no lies). It took extreme obedience for two people to connect through the gossip, the obvious, the lies, the scandals, the sin, the past relationships, and the drama to make it against all odds. Some are still watching and waiting for the destruction and that moment they can say "Ah ha, I told you," "Oh she's just with him for his money," "Oh, he's just with her for her looks". To know us is to know we both come with a lot of "STUFF"; things, neither money nor looks could survive! BUT GOD! He used our union to redeem us BOTH! And to bring us both out together! Just like any other married couple, you learn pretty quickly that marriage is WORK! In this relationship, I have learned A LOT of lessons, but the blessing in it is that I've LEARNED and the results have been more than I could have ever imagined! God showed me that everything started with ME, which trickled down to all of my relationship(s). Since walking through these studies and following careful instruction, my husband has been AMAZING to say the least. He is more attentive, loving, and more calm. We are becoming who God ordained for us to be to each other! And as for Diane, the wife—I have changed, I see him as powerful, more assertive. I view him as the head, as a provider, and so much more. I didn't know I could love him any more than I already did, but God has opened my heart up to receive and give so much more than I could ever imagine. Now trust me there is still A LOT and I do mean A LOT of work to be done but what God has joined together, let NO man separate! (**Matthew 19:6**). Diane the mother has learned to let go. All of our children have become Adults and now have to use what they were taught—prayer, scripture, relationship, and developing their own walk and talk with God, and when they fall and fail to love them through it! *Love is AGAPE!!! (**1 Corinthians 13:4-8**).

PC: I Promise you if you Continue with the Plan, your Entire Household will fall in line!! See God works on everything and everybody but it's all in Order and it's All Working for Your Good!! If you just Follow the Instructions that God gives me for you you'll be shouting everyday! It started with getting you back to your Rightful Place in God! Victor is already feeling a Greater Appreciation for You his WIFE & LIFE PARTNER, soon you'll be able to experience the JOY of each of your Children not only Appreciating You but Connecting with You!! Just be Patient and Follow the Instructions.

✠✠✠

Chapter VII: Level UP!

Level #1: Home is where the Heart is!

To PC: This morning, I just spent time in God's face just listening. Yesterday, Genesis was complaining about pains in her stomach so she went to bed early. This morning, while in prayer, God instructed me to anoint my hands with oil; He said: Go upstairs, touch her head and stomach, and claim healing and protection over her body in Jesus' name. I knew this would be uncomfortable for both of us but I did as instructed. As I did this, she looked confused but allowed me to do what I did. You see my kids know that their mother is a prayer warrior, they've heard me pray for others, seen me pray, know I had a prayer email devotional that reached hundreds around the world. I've prayed with them and always for them but this was different; to speak to their sickness while touching them was foreign for me and them! When I came back downstairs, God said to me, "*IT STARTS AT HOME! IF YOU CANNOT HEAL YOUR FAMILY, THEN HOW CAN YOU HEAL OTHERS?!*" I think of so many Pastors/Prophets, etc. that help the world but can't help their own family or their household is suffering from neglect and weakness because "we" feel like at home we can "be ourselves/relax" as if the power turns off at home and our family doesn't need help or healing.

As I continued to be still and listen, this is what the Lord said to me: *I HAVE TO BE YOUR ONLY RESOURCE OVER ANY AND ALL ISSUES. YOU SHOULD EAGERLY BE READY TO GIVE (SICKNESS, ISSUES, PROBLEMS, ANYTHING) TO THE ONE WHO CAN FIX IT! I AM THE WAY, THE TRUTH, AND THE LIFE, I AM THE HEALER AND THE PHYSICIAN. TRUST ME TO DO IT FOR YOU. I WILL DO IT FOR YOU, DIANE! BELIEVE IN ME BEYOND YOUR THOUGHTS, LOGIC, AND INTELLECT. I WILL DO THIS WITH RECKLESS ABANDONMENT; I WILL DO THIS AS THE WIND BLOWS. I AM UNPREDICTABLE YET FAITHFUL! I AM MOVING IN YOU AND WITH YOU DIFFERENTLY. EYES HAVE NOT SEEN WHAT I WILL ACCOMPLISH IN AND THROUGH YOU. TRUST AND MOVE MY DAUGHTER!*

God, let your will be done! Holy Spirit, I give you full reign, lead me and guide me! I come to do your will!

PC's Response: WOW a Great Lesson to start your day with! It's imperative that we learn the importance of the Home Being Healthy in all areas! You're right, so many Leaders are more concerned with healing the nations and their own home is plagued with the sickness of all forms!! You're swimming in deep water now!

Level #2: I am Human!

After a misunderstanding with my husband and not being able to decipher what was wrong with him, I conceded and left his workplace but my heart was wounded, my mind was racing, and my emotions were VERY unstable. I went home and couldn't do anything but cry, pray, praise, cry some more, and praise again because I refused to let the enemy get me. I PRAYED over my marriage, my husband, myself, our bed, EVERYTHING, and I went to sleep! This morning during prayer I lifted everything up. God revealed some things to me and gave me peace!

My Prayer: Oh God, I thank you for being the lifter of my downcast spirit! Thank you for making sense of what I am feeling, and most importantly thank you for giving me discernment that I can understand the place that my husband is in. This is what the Lord said to me: *MY DAUGHTER, I AM IN CONTROL OF EVERYTHING! I LOVE YOU AND I CARE ABOUT EVERY DETAIL OF YOUR LIFE. DO NOT LET THE THINGS THAT "I" AM WORKING OUT IN YOUR HUSBAND CAUSE YOU TO LOSE HEART. HE NEEDS YOU! HE NEEDS YOUR STRENGTH, YOUR COURAGE, YOUR PRAYERS, YOUR SUPPORT, YOUR UNDERSTANDING, AND, MOST IMPORTANTLY, YOUR LOVE! I AM IN CONTROL. DO NOT FAINT OR GET WEARY IN WELL DOING, YOU WILL REAP THIS HARVEST! NOT EVERYTHING IS AN ATTACK; SOME THINGS NEED TO BE UPROOTED IN ORDER FOR HEALTHY SEEDS TO BE PLANTED. YOU AND YOUR HUSBAND WILL BEAR MUCH FRUIT! I LOVE YOU, MY CHILD, AND YOU ARE STRONG ENOUGH TO ENDURE THIS SHIFT!*

What God showed me about ME: My unstable emotions stem from my past, not receiving the love I desired as a child and holding my husband accountable for it!. THIS NEEDS TO BE DEALT WITH!!!!

PC's Response: Yes, we must address these emotional issues! Because you almost went into Burnout mode!! You had forgotten what God has constantly told you and that is HE'S GOT YOU AND YOU WILL NOT FAIL!! I need you to become more Stable; you can't become unglued at the sight of Adversity! Now as far as Victor goes, he needs to hear you say, "I LOVE YOU AND EVERYTHING IS GOING TO BE ALRIGHT!! WE'RE IN THIS TOGETHER!" This is something that you need to say to him IMMEDIATELY! So take a break and call him NOW!! You can't be his Strength and you're Weak! Now as far as your Emotions go, you've got to DISCIPLINE YOURSELF to a point where you are TOTALLY CONVINCED IN GOD'S PROMISES TO YOU! And which means that you're going to have to Learn how to Control your Emotions! Your Emotions respond to what you See! So we must begin Immediately working on your PERCEPTION!!

My Response: I believe there is a trigger. It's the same thing always when I am rejected and have no control over it; mostly I can accept rejection IF I did something to deserve it (and it almost makes me want to do something to deserve it). Also, it is only triggered during a specific time of the month when my body is purging.

PC's Response: News Flash—it shouldn't matter what time of the month it is or what the conditions are, YOU HAVE TO CONTROL YOUR EMOTIONS AND ENVIRONMENT!! Your PERCEPTION of Rejection is WRONG! If Jesus was Rejected so will we be, but He didn't lose Focus on the PLAN! AND NEITHER SHOULD YOU!! You Immediately allow Rejection to control your Emotions, and then your Emotions lead to the Basement! If you plan on staying and Enjoying the Ocean, then you're going to have to see Rejection differently.

My Response: I'm NOT losing focus!!! I FELT something. I felt HURT (I am human) just as Jesus did even with him knowing he had to go through what he went through, even knowing he would rise from the death he would go through, he still felt pain, he still cried, he still felt hurt; no he didn't give up and neither will I!

I did not stay there. Yes, I cried but I prayed! Yes, I felt rejected but I immediately went into praise! Yes, I was upset with how my husband treated me unjustly! But I still lifted him/us and our marriage up in prayer EVEN with feeling emotional! Yes, I am willing to look at and work on the feelings of rejection; I am glad it is EXPOSED because it NEEDED to come out so now it's out.

Since I have been under your mentor-ship, I have done EVERYTHING you have asked me to do (even in some cases with a fight lol). All of which created an atmosphere to be treated the way I should have been treated from the start! I have been asked to overlook my husband's faults, encourage him, pray for him, care about his feelings, care about his dreams, wants, desires, etc., and I have been doing just that! On the flip side of this, I have been blessed with a rekindled relationship with God, peace, and joy in my heart, and a new zeal to FIGHT and stay in the fight. I know God has more. I am expecting more. Trust me I am not going backward. God allows things to come out in order to deal with them.

But it's confusing when I'm being told to overlook my feelings, toughen up, ignore what I feel, stop being emotional and yet I have to coddle my husband's feelings, be understanding of his faults and his emotions, pay attention to the same feelings in him that I FEEL! That is why I'm so confused because when all of what I am doing for him/us/our marriage is draining for me; I have no one to encourage me in the same way with (understanding)!

I know I am strong. God encourages me in it every day so spiritually I get it. But sometimes (just sometimes) the human side needs a little nudge, not a shove!

PC's Response: It appears at times like now that it's one-sided, but the Encouragement You Receive from God should cover you Spiritually and Physically. However, you've only been Receiving it for your Spiritual Man and haven't allowed your Natural Man to enjoy or benefit from it! Diane, you are not just a normal woman with an Anointing, God has a Greater Purpose for your Life and at times it can feel very Lonely! But you've got to see what God is going to do through you! You are Learning and Growing!! You will soon get past this too! It can be difficult being the Strength of a Family, the Tie that Binds, the Connector that keeps a Family Connected to God, but be reassured that no one else could do it if so He would have

Ordained them to do it! A while ago, I Welcomed you to my World, now you're truly feeling what I and those like us feel daily! We have to Sacrifice so much so often but we were Chosen for this!! Christ felt what we often feel that's why He cried out "My God Why Have You Forsaken Me!" Many are Called but few are Chosen; we've been Chosen! And oftentimes, we have to overlook our own needs of Comfort and Encouragement for the Greater Good. But God reassures us it's all Worth It!!

My Response: I absolutely get what you're saying and definitely agree! I have been overlooking and ignoring my feelings ever since I can remember; I have always put other people's feelings above my own. It's not new for me or a struggle, it's second nature. God has ALWAYS been there for me emotionally/physically; I have felt his presence and nothing and no one will ever supersede that! I can remember me crying alone MANY times with visions of me laying on his lap, with him stroking my hair, comforting me in my deepest and darkest despair! I don't want to be told to just ignore what I'm feeling;

I want to learn how to FIGHT! Because I am different, my emotions could take me OUT, and I want to LIVE!

Level #3: I am a Woman Hear me ROAR!

To PC: I had an encounter last night. While I was at choir rehearsal, I began to have a severe headache; one that I've never had before. It was brief but strange. When I got home and spoke to my husband on the phone, he didn't sound good. He expressed he's been having a severe headache all day off and on (he assumes it's the allergies). I said that explains what I was feeling. I prayed and told him he needs to go get a checkup. He stayed at the yard that night so I called him this morning, he said it is a little better. My prayer today was that God would ease his pain but put a fire under his feet to get his physical done. I cannot babysit and hold his hand but I keep encouraging him to take care of his body which helps him make his livelihood and his source of income. One of the hardest things for us to do is to take the time to take care of ourselves until it's too late and we are forced to do it!

All of our adult children are moving back to Georgia one by one and they are pulling at him. He expressed to me yesterday that it was part of the reason we had our disagreement because he had a lot of that on his mind. I do my best to keep things in perspective because I refuse for ANYONE to take advantage of him; I am VERY protective of him because I know he could easily be persuaded into things when people are persistent in what they're trying to get out of him.

PC's Response: You must be his emotional Strength during this time. The enemy is attacking him Emotionally and Mentally; trying to break him. He's under attack and he doesn't understand why, so soothe his Emotions as only Wife Diane can do. Then he'll relax, breathe, and the Holy Spirit will intervene.

My Response: Now you know I am looking at this side-eyed. These are the same attacks that were affecting MY emotions. This stuff is wearing me out! I know I am strong but good God GEESE!!! I'm feeling a double standard here!

PC: You have a Great responsibility, both Naturally and Spiritually! But this comes with who you are. You wanted what God had for you, you wanted to be God's Diane. Well with all of that Favor, Being Chosen, and of Course, Being

Spoiled, also comes Work, Strenuous Work, Self-Sacrifice, and an Abundance of Responsibilities.

My Response: I have absolutely no problem with all of that but when I EMOTIONALLY break down or as you said about my husband, I am being "attacked," I don't want to be treated like Teflon. I want to be told, "I understand, let's work through this thing, you can do this, it's OK TO CRY IT OUT, come on get back in the rink!" I am not even looking for all of the MUSH. I have to give to my husband to coddle his emotions but just understanding.

PC: Yes, OK, well, I Understand; It's OK to Cry. Get Back in The Rink; You're A Winner. NOW YOU'RE COVERED, FOR THE NEXT TIME JUST REREAD THIS MESSAGE LOL.

My Response: OMG!!! That was like PULLING TEETH!!!! You have to understand although I am strong I am watching EVERYTHING, I am being taught, and if I notice double standards, especially with you being a man teaching a woman, then I am going to HAVE to say something because I don't want it to create in me ill feelings toward my husband. I don't want to see my husband as weak and myself as strong. I want us both to win so as I fight for him I need YOU to fight for ME!!!So that I can stay in the rink!

PC: So now I've got to Fight for you?? Pray for you, pray with you, mentor you, be your Instructor, etc. This is becoming way too difficult. I prefer just being Genesis Godfather lol. By the way, you'll never see your husband as weak as long as you're under my tutelage; not Going to Happen!! He's got to be strong to deal with you. Besides you should know by now I'm about Order!! And that's out of Order. I couldn't Mentor a Woman who couldn't see and Honor her husband's Strength! Because she couldn't hear me if she couldn't hear her husband! You have a new nickname, Mrs. Teflon!! Lol, and for the record, if you stay Focused on my Directions, you won't have time to worry about your feelings. Plus I'm a Warrior Trainer, we eat emotions for breakfast lol.

My Response: (laughing out loud!) Mrs. Teflon and TRUST my husband is BLESSED BEYOND BLESSED. I am nothing like any other woman that he could have ended up with! Especially with how I've been treated and I STILL LOVE HIM more than ever!! Not because of the way he treats me but because GOD placed that love in me specifically for him. As for my feelings: I'm trying to tell you we, women, have emotions too, just don't ignore them; acknowledge they exist and move on and we will be happy, but don't dismiss them!

PC: I don't see gender with y'all. I only see People that God has entrusted to my care! Lol.

My Response: Well therein lies the problem!!!! Let me help you out then!!! I, (Us) women, are not just any other "people"! I am Deborah, Ruth, Esther, Mary, Hannah, Zelophehad's daughters! I am Woman, Hear Me ROAR!

Level #4: Your Tears!

Tears Well up: To gradually or steadily flow upwards or outwards so as to begin to fill or overflow something, literally or figuratively. To begin to form tears. The unfinished stage of crying; water begins to accumulate within the eyes

Study from John 4 (Samaritan woman at the Well)—Being "at the well" allows me to be vulnerable, all of my sins, flaws, emotional breakdowns lol, STUFF lay bare before Jesus, who does not condemn me, nor does he dismiss my vulnerable state but he gets me to acknowledge the ugly truth! Then he is able to give me exactly what I need to get better (living water). This gives me the desire to take everything I learn back to my family in words, deeds, spirit, emotions, and actions! We do what we are taught; Jesus taught in meekness yet with authority and boldness, calling out what he already knew—allowing us to be honest and truthful with him. The Pharisees and Sadducees were taught the harsh reality of the law and thus they held everyone (including Jesus) to that same standard of harshness. My desire is to learn how to bring out the best in others while they are in their "WELL" state.

✠✠✠

Poem: In the Wells of the Eyes

In the wells of her eyes, I could see the water overflowing.

Capturing a cupful, I was able to see into her heart;

her pain, her cares, her heartache, her fears

All found in just one teardrop

In the wells of his eyes, he looked up to keep the water from falling

But I could still see into his soul

The lids unable to take the pressure began to release his frustrations

His doubts, his struggles, his anger, his troubles, all relied on him controlling the teardrops

But the control lies in the hands of the creator.

Tears were given as a weapon against the enemy called pride

Tears were given to reveal the things we try to hide

In the wells of the eyes deep down in the ducts of our spirit, we are able to cry! ©DJ 11/9/07

For the Lamb at the center of the throne will be their shepherd; 'he will lead them to springs of living water'. 'And God will wipe away every tear from their eyes' (**Revelation 7:17**).

Level #4: I See You!

Encounter (6:03 a.m.): I was putting on my face lotion (in the dark because my husband was still sleeping). As I was looking in my mirror I saw it standing behind me in my room. A demonic spirit—tall in stature, black, burnt face, horns, ridged teeth, very angry; just huffing, and intensely staring at me through the mirror. I had absolutely NO FEAR when I saw it. In my mind, I said, "I see you." I began praising God (under my breath) for his protection over my life, and I thanked him for his host of angels that encamp around me so that I do not dash my foot against the stone. I then spoke directly to it; "By the blood of Jesus (it trembled), I command you to go back to the pit of hell where you came from; I bind you NEVER to return again!" It disappeared! I then praised God again for his angels that protect me daily. I then saw two giant angels standing tall at attention resting their hands on their swords; ready and alert! I turned around to face their direction and said, "Thank you, Gabriel and Michael, for your return, and thank you host of angels that continue to watch over me and my family!" I finished putting on my lotion with a smile!!! **Psalm 91:11-12**

Level #5: A Father's Influence!

PC: The Holy Spirit said to me in prayer this morning to Speak to You, so I want you to know that I Love You as my Daughter and Student. You have Grown in so many ways in areas that you aren't even aware of and in areas that you may think that I'm unaware of!! The Holy Spirit showed me how God has Disciplined you in your Time with Him and even with your Finances. I saw your Seed Jars, First Fruit and the Victory jar, and they're Growing and you have Learned the importance of your Love to your Husband, you've closed a gap between you and your children, and now you've launched out in the ocean and begun swimming! You're soon to be a Published Author, you've allowed your Gift of song to Bless all who hear it, and so much more!! Diane, I'm Proud of You, and it's a joy fathering and Mentoring You!!!

My Response: Thank you for this encouragement! You must have heard my heart this morning. While driving to work I was listening to the radio and as each radio personality spoke highly of what their fathers taught them, they asked people who called in to give one example of an influence their father had on them. Although my dad is in my life today and we have a wonderful, healthy, and happy functioning relationship, I grew up without that constant reality in my household as a child and I looked for it in every male figure I encountered; so I couldn't think of an influential memory that I could relate to. So then I thought of YOU. I said, "Well, I have a spiritual dad who is here and who has influenced me today!!!!" and then I get this text from you....

PC's Response: Lol stop trying to make me cry because it's working!

Chapter VIII: Facing the Jezebel Spirit!

My Study on **1 Kings 21**

What do you believe the characteristics of the Jezebel Spirit are?

*Bitterness toward men

*Male bashing–speaking ill about men or your man!

*Understating a man's worth and/or value—the I don't need a man syndrome!

*Taking away their power and control—belittling their ability

What do/did you see in yourself: Not being "Godly" submissive in my role as a wife, meaning undermining my husband's decisions because I think I have a better way and although my way is better at times I still FAIL the test because I am out of God's divine order!

Lesson: I have learned that God has to work in my husband too and if I take away his lessons by doing everything for him then we both fail the test!

Confession: I am in debt now from doing just that, instead of being persistent in my asking due to my needs or patiently waiting for my husband to do it; I said, "If you want something done, you got to do it yourself"! So I convinced myself to buy whatever "I" needed to fix the things MY HUSBAND should have been fixing. I let him off the hook and put myself into severe debt. The oops in all of this is #1 he didn't even know I (WE) were going into debt, #2 I had the arrogant attitude of I don't need your money or your skills, I can do it myself! *Part of this was anger; I was angry that he didn't choose to make sure our home was taken care of; I felt like we were not a priority. But I also didn't realize I had already made him feel like an outsider by taking his power in the home! Woo wee Jesus fix it! So he adopted an AHAB spirit and I adopted a JEZEBEL spirit! Good God! Completely OUT OF ORDER! Thank you, God, for correction!!!!

PC's Response: The Holy Spirit Just Released this to me, *YOU HADN'T ALLOWED HIM TO LOVE YOU FULLY AND THIS WAS ONE OF THE PROBLEMS! YOU WERE TRYING TO DO TOO MUCH!!!! STOP IT! YOU HAVE TO LET HIM PROVIDE FOR YOU, TREAT YOU, SPOIL YOU!! WHEN YOU DON'T ALLOW HIM TO DO THESE THINGS, IT TAKES SOMETHING OUT OF HIM!!! I REBUKE THAT SPIRIT OF CONTROL!!! STOP TRYING TO MAKE*

EVERYTHING EASY FOR EVERYONE, MEN NEED TO FEEL THAT THEY'RE NEEDED!!! WE WERE DESIGNED TO SOLVE PROBLEMS!!!!

My Response: Yes, Sir, I hear you loud and clear. For years I was attempting to do EVERYTHING in the hopes to prove my love to my husband and to show him I wasn't trying to use him for money and I didn't realize I was causing more problems than a few! I can only blame myself for where we were! Since identifying these errors I had to:

First, identify the spirits in the home and then kick them out!!! This took careful instruction from the Holy Spirit, prayer oil, fasting and prayer. Paying close attention to the characteristics I display so that I do not invite her back into my home.

Second, be patient in the process because God has to work in BOTH of us to slowly correct and repair the damage done. I have a new found respect for my husband and although he is still slow to do the things needing to be fixed in the home, I now TRUST GOD to teach him the lesson that's needed! God was always waiting on ME!

PC's Response: Good! Take Ownership!! We get impatient then we start our own plan, that's what gets us in trouble all the time! Most women fail to understand that they strip the Man of his Responsibilities trying to help or wanting things done on their time schedule but when they do this it only creates a problem later! I'm happy that these lessons are Allowing you to see what God has brought you through and now you're able to help other women navigate through these difficult Waters.

✠✠✠

Chapter IX: Jezebel Goes to Church!

For so it was, while Jezebel massacred the prophets of the Lord, that Obadiah had taken one hundred prophets and hidden them, fifty to a cave, and had fed them with bread and water. (**1 Kings 18:4**).

The Jezebel spirit is running rampant in the church. Some so debilitating it causes "church hurt."

When I pray I've learned to call out the tentacles/attachments of a spirit which God showed me concerns the "emotions" of a spirit (i.e. depression, greed, Bipolar-ism, fear, discord, jealousy, lust, insecurity, shame, etc.) but God also has me calling out the ROOT of the spirit (molestation, sin, abuse, broken spirit, rejection, etc.) And the only way to do this is to know which spiritual entity/host is at work (i.e., Jezebel, Ahab, Delilah, Belial, Pharoah, Baal, Beelzebub, etc.). Under these spirits become the acts associated with them (fornication, poor eating habits, lying, stealing, murder, promiscuity, suicide, etc.). These spirits are on the rise to attack and kill the Prophets and the people of the church! Jezebel is one of those spirits assigned to the Prophets! This is not done literally but subtly;

these spirits are planted in the church, ministries, prayer groups, and right next to the Bishop(s)/Pastor(s) of the house! They come to attack seasoned Prophets and to Kill the spirit of developing Prophets and Saints. Most will not venture too close to a seasoned Prophet because they KNOW that they can be exposed so they get in the Pastor's ear and they work to diminish the character of a person. This is why you have fifteen-plus Ministers on a church roster and you only hear from a selected few, because the Jezebel spirit has already influenced the decisions of a Pastor about others so they fail to use them for anything! Eventually, these Ministers end up leaving the church to go elsewhere preaching from a wounded place; thus attracting and creating MORE Jezebels into their congregations! I have seen this so many times in different churches!!! Others never come to their full potential; these are the "cave dwellers," still hiding their gifting because of the threat of Jezebel!

As a person coming into their gifting, you always want to be acknowledged by your Spiritual Leader, you want to have confirmation of what God showed you about yourself but unfortunately most Pastors are either not gifted with that discernment or never get close enough to a person to identify their abilities and/or power, which is why the "Prophets" are needed. These are people who God gifted with the anointing to spiritually see a person's abilities, not taking a "gifting" test but God revealing the unknown to them in order for them to help develop the Saints. These are the ones the Pastors need to have around them but once again the Jezebels quickly plant themselves in position; ready and waiting to assassinate the prophets!

PC's Response: WOW this is really good, that's why this study is so powerful and prevalent!! It camouflages itself well, and because most people don't know it's Traits or it's characteristics, it comes right into their Lives, Homes, Relationships, Churches, and Ministries.

My Response: My entire body is stirring up!!! Like EVERYTHING IS SPIRITUAL! I can remember when I first surrendered and moved to GA, I use to watch a prominent Pastor on TV; I was fascinated with the level of anointing he had on him and how God moved mightily in his ministry, people were being healed just by being present! Most are skeptical to these kinds of practices but I KNEW it was real!!! I have not seen this level of power in ANY church I have ever visited. Yet this is the level of power we are supposed to be displaying in ALL of God's dwelling places!!! So many of God's people walking around sick in their bodies, broke, in bondage to something, lazy, jealous, confused, backbiting, etc. We have NO power whatsoever inside of the buildings because these spirits are running rampant! That's why God said to me, "It's not enough to call out "feelings/emotions," we have to expose the actual host/root!"

Question: *What Spirit are you dealing with; within your church, in your home, at your job? CALL IT OUT! Do not allow it to harm another person you claim to care about! Once you expose it. CAST IT OUT!!!

Prayer: Father, God, in the name of Jesus, I bind every spiritual tentacle, vein, vessel, thought, action, generational curse, emotional attack that comes from the spirit of Jezebel, the spirit of Ahab, the spirit of Delilah, the spirit of Beelzebub, the spirit of Pharaoh, and the likes there of I call out every characteristic plague to create bondage in our lives, and I cast them into the lake of fire, never to return! God, your word says that we have the power to tear down imaginations, and every high thing that exalts itself against your knowledge, to bring into captivity every thought to the obedience to Christ. We ask that you EXPOSE this spirit, bring everything it does to the surface, and give every Pastor the eyes to see these impostors for who they are. Help them to identify the character traits so that not another person under their care gets hurt! And Oh God, protect their minds, their hearts, their emotions, and their deposit. It's in Jesus' name we pray, Amen!

✠✠✠

Chapter X: The Frenemies of Jezebel!

Frenemy: Someone who pretends to be your friend, but is really your enemy.

*The enemy of my enemy is my friend.

So today God had me looking at "frenemies"; I personally do not have any in my life but I have encountered some over the years!

1 Kings 21 (Key Verses 8-10): 8 So Jezebel wrote letters in Ahab's name, placed his seal on them, and sent them to the elders and nobles who lived in Naboth's city with him. 9 In those letters she wrote: "Proclaim a day of fasting and seat Naboth in a prominent place among the people. 10 *But seat two scoundrels opposite him and have them bring charges that he has cursed both God and the king. Then take him out and stone him to death*."

Lesson: Make sure you know who's seated at the table! If David said in **Psalm 23:5a**, You prepare a table before me in the presence of my enemies then why do "we think" everyone with us is for us? Jezebel used a "fast" as a trap in order to lie on Naboth and accuse him of cursing God. (As if that bothered her.) All to take something she wanted for her own scheme!

When someone wants what you have they will pretend to have your best interest at heart only to get you set up! These Jezebels don't care about you personally, you just have something they want and/or something that can further their agenda! And in our hunger and desire to fit into the "in crowd," we welcome them with open arms. They join our prayer groups, show up at our meetings, break bread with us only to take what we have, and assassinate our character! This is prevalent at our jobs, ministries, relationships, etc. Before we know it, we've given them all of our secrets; they know our vulnerabilities and what makes us "tick," and before we know it they are sharing it with the world! There is a saying: if you want to keep a secret do not tell ANYBODY! Once you tell one person, it's no longer a secret!

Confession #1: There are some things that I will take to my grave! But there are times when I came very close to telling people who I thought were my friends and after exposing them for the impostors that they were, I would breathe a sigh of relief. WHEW! So glad I didn't tell them that! Because in anger the flesh has a tendency to not only spread lies but reveal your truth—your most vulnerable, sensitive digressions that you may have disclosed in an effort to confess, heal, and/or be delivered from past pain, hurt, abuse, or sins!

Confession #2: There have been times in my life where I have been jealous or coveted something a CORE friend had (yes I said the "J" word!); not to the extent of harming them in any way but just desiring to be in their shoes for that moment for what I believed at that time to be a better comfortable pair. So if "I" being a genuine friend have felt this way about true friendships then imagine what a frenemy could do disguised as someone you deem to be worthy of your inner circle???! I have this intuition within my friend zone; if you can talk unfavorable about one of our core friends to me, then I KNOW you are talking about me to them. This is when you must evaluate your own authenticity to those you call "bestie," or brother, or "sis". This is when you search your own inner self for that hidden "J" word!

*The enemy of my enemy is my friend, but are they really?

As believers, we get too comfortable with our surroundings and in the name of "keeping it real," "being transparent," or desperately wanting to fit in, we give power to those who really don't even like us and want what we have! They are "naysayers" planted by the enemy to take our deposit! We don't even realize it is a spiritual attack, character assassination, and is designed to tarnish our reputation so that our witness becomes ineffective! Once again the Jezebel spirit doing what it was designed to do!!!

PC's Response: Wow, now this will Preach! Very good OBSERVATION and transparency!! You're really getting to the Root of this study.

My Response: This study has helped me be more discerning of who I call "friend" as well as it helps me check my own character to see if I am displaying Jezebel traits!

Proverbs 16:28

A perverse person stirs up conflict, and a gossip separates close friends.

Chapter XI: Visions, Dreams, and His Voice!

"In the last days, God says, I will pour out my Spirit on all people. Your sons and daughters will prophesy, your young men will see visions, your old men will dream dreams." (**Acts 2:17**).

In this chapter, God is dealing with me regarding my visions, dreams, revelation. It wasn't until several years ago that I realized I had the gift of vision and dreams. I concluded that I must have eaten something late at night and just brushed them off. Hindsight as I look back to when I first surrendered, God had been attempting to speak to me through visions for over 20+ years; so now I've learned to write down EVERYTHING I was seeing and then wait and listen for God's still small voice to speak to my heart! So God asked me this question.

Question: *IN YOUR MIND'S EYES, WHAT DO YOU SEE BY FAITH?* As I closed my eyes I begin to see the following:

What I was seeing VS what it meant to me…

-God's hands reaching out to me: God's safety **Isaiah 59:1**

-Chariots, horses, hosts of angels: Armies getting prepared for a battle! **Revelation 19:19**

-Fire: God's presence **Exodus 13:21**

-Smiles and laughter: my feelings **Psalm 126:2-3**

-My Journals: The promises of God: **2 Corinthians 1:20**

-Bright ball of light; God's Power **Genesis 1:3**

-Resolve: calmness, God's peace **Philippians 4:7**

-Anointing flowing from my fingertips: my gifting

1Corinthians 12:7-11

-Animals of all kind praising God in his presence; his sovereignty **Psalm 148**

-Colors, vibrant, deep, rich: Heaven! **Revelation 4**

*The gifting of vision and revelation are subjected to scrutiny, doubt, misunderstanding, and disbelief! Not just by the receiver but also by the person seeing the vision.

*Not everyone can handle your gift. Sometimes you can't even handle it and you allow doubt and fear to hinder or distort what God is giving and showing you!

In **Acts 25** —David said this about God: "I saw the Lord always before me. Because he is at my right hand, I will not be shaken."

Picturing things that God says are true using the eyes of faith. David saw the reality by setting the Lord at his right hand. So King David used the eyes of his heart and practiced Godly imagination; pictures on his mind and in his heart that God used to communicate his truth to him! David then made it a reality in his life by how he responded to his turmoil! I WILL NOT BE SHAKEN! This takes FAITH! There are times by faith when I NEED to see God; and there are times when God opens my eyes to his understanding and he draws a picture before me of what he wants me to see!

Observation: Over the years, God has used visions and dreams to show me what he was going to do in and through me; nothing I could physically do on my own but supernatural things. Up until now, I could not grasp these revelations because of all of the doubt, fear, and disbelief. But God has been confirming all that he's said to me by strengthening me and imprinting it on my heart and the manifestations of what I am seeing physically and spiritually ARE REAL IN MY MIND AND HEART AND SO SHALL BE IN MY PHYSICAL REALM AND SPIRITUAL REALM!!! THIS IS

DECLARED AND DECREED FROM THIS DAY FORWARD! These are some of the encounters through visions and dreams that I have experienced over the years.

Glass Half Empty or Glass Half Full?

7:30 p.m.: As I listened to my worship music the song "YES" was on. As I worshiped, I saw a vision of a glass full of water; in the water were black dirt particles. I began to see water being poured into the glass until the water overflowed. As it spilled out it began to get completely clear until there were no more dirt particles left in the cup! I asked, "God, what does this mean?" He said: *DIANE, I WILL POUR INTO YOU ALL THAT I HAVE UNTIL WHAT IS IN YOU THAT IS NOT LIKE ME WILL BE REMOVED. YOU MUST STAY OPEN TO RECEIVE. STAY FOCUSED, STAY ALERT! THIS WILL BE DONE IN INTERVALS YOU CANNOT HANDLE IT ALL AT ONCE. REMAIN IN ANTICIPATION, READY TO RECEIVE; I WILL FILL YOU UP. I KNOW IT APPEARS AS THOUGH THE CUP IS ALREADY FULL AS THOUGH THERE IS NO MORE ROOM TO RECEIVE BUT I AM PROVIDING YOU WITH OVERFLOW! YOU WILL NO LONGER GIVE OUT OF*

AN EMPTY PLACE; YOU WILL NO LONGER GIVE OUT OF BROKENNESS. YOU WILL GIVE OUT OF AN ABUNDANCE OF WHAT I PLACE IN YOU. YOU ARE CLEAN!!! (**Psalm 23:5**).

I have Chosen You!

Vision: I was standing in the middle of a field with a long flowing dress on; it was raining. I just stood in the middle of the field embracing the rain, dancing, twirling, and spinning. I began to smile because I knew the rain was washing some things away!

7:41 p.m.: While I was recording everything I was seeing, it was actually thundering and raining outside!!!

As I continued to worship, God's presence began to overwhelm me. I had an intense desire for him to draw near to me! I began to weep; I said, "God who am I that you would choose me???"

Vision 2: I see coal being placed on my lips! I asked the Lord, "What does this mean?" He said: *I SHALL PLACE MY WORDS IN YOUR MOUTH; YOU WILL SPEAK FOR ME. I HAVE CHOSEN YOU, DIANE!*

I begin to shake and cry out of fear. God interrupted me with his peace. He said to me: *DO NOT FEAR FOR I AM WITH YOU. I WILL GIVE YOU EVERYTHING YOU NEED TO PROCEED! IT WILL BE ME WORKING THROUGH YOU. DO NOT WORRY ABOUT WHAT NEEDS TO BE SAID JUST STAY READY AND LISTEN FOR MY VOICE; YOU WILL KNOW IT IS ME*! (**John 10:27**).

Vision 3: I saw myself dancing in the rain again. I began to run with all my might toward this bright light. God gave me **Isaiah 6**!

PC's Response: I knew this was going to be good because you never email me this late lol and I was correct!! Another Level, Growth and Promotion all at the same time!! Now get ready to Work!

There's a Word that will Burn within your belly until you release it!! Yes, all things are Working Together for Your Good!! Just don't stop Receiving! Proud of You!!

The Anointing Power of God!

Encounter (6:39 a.m.): As I prayed and anointed myself:

Head—Remove impure thoughts and help me to think about what is good and true

Eyes—To see the beauty of your world; to see like you, Lord, and to see into your Spirit Realm

Ears—To hear your voice that I may know your commands and ears to listen to the hearts of mankind

Nose—To sense when you are near; the sweet aroma of your presence

Mouth—To speak with grace and boldness in and out of season

Throat—To anoint my vocal cords so that every note is sung precisely with healing power, deliverance and the wind of my voice will set the captives free

Heart—To feel compassion and love

Stomach—To discern the presence of the Holy Spirit

Feet—To MOVE as guided and to move quickly by faith and not by sight

Hands—To bless everything I touch with whatever is needed for them; to allow the power to flow freely!!!

As I closed my eyes and worshiped, I lifted up my hands to receive God's power. I said, "God I lift my hands up to receive! Two beams of light poured out from them. I opened my mouth to praise Him for what I was receiving; light beamed out of my mouth! I said: "God, what does this mean?"

He said to me: *I HAVE GIVEN YOU MY POWER, NOW WALK IN IT! YOU HAD NOT BECAUSE YOU ASKED NOT. BUT TODAY YOU HAVE ASKED SO YOU HAVE RECEIVED. ANYTHING YOU ASK IN MY NAME FROM THIS DAY FORWARD YOU SHALL RECEIVE BY FAITH! MY DAUGHTER, WITH ME YOU CAN MOVE MOUNTAINS, WITH ME NOTHING IS IMPOSSIBLE FOR THOSE WHO BELIEVE! DO YOU BELIEVE YOU HAVE RECEIVED THIS?* I said, "YES, DADDY!!!!" (**Matthew 17:20**).

As I began to pray, God showed me one of my friends. I was to bless them. I began to speak in tongues calling out their name. I was instructed to touch them and bless them with God's peace. They were grieving; I talk to them often reassuring them that God is still on the throne. I dare not tell them I understand their pain nor do I tell them how long they should take with the grieving process.

As I was given these instructions, I thought of my son who is struggling emotionally again. I can always tell because of his mood changes INSTANTLY (a mother always knows when her children are struggling internally). Anyway, I thought to myself I could touch him and he will receive peace as well. But when I thought of going upstairs to touch him I could see the power cut off. God told me, "NOT NOW"! I said, "Yes, Lord, I understand, it's not time." I put my friend back in my mind again and the power in my hands came back on. This is for THEM!

I got to my destination and went straight to them; I hugged my friend tightly and blessed them with God's peace. They said, "THANK YOU" with a big smile; "I sure did need that today." I said, "HE KNEW you needed it!" And I ran to my errand.

PC's Response: Another Level Gained! Yes, where you are now is a delicate place and it must be guarded and highly regarded!! You must work on this Level with TIMING and POSITIONING!! Because when it's TIME to RELEASE this

OIL/POWER, IT MUST ONLY BE RELEASED ON THOSE THAT IT IS PURPOSED FOR AT THE DESIGNATED TIME AND PLACE! God has put you in a place very Few are allowed. In this place, you also MUST MOVE WHEN INSTRUCTED TO, because PEOPLE'S LIVES ARE DEPENDING ON IT! I'm honored to be sharing this place with you!! As I have said to you previously, WELCOME TO MY WORLD! As much as we desire to share this ANOINTING with Family, we can't unless specifically instructed to by our Father because it can harm them if they're not properly prepared to Receive it. My prayer is that you come to learn the importance of this peculiar Gift! Many will want to deplete you of it because they can see it!! And it's very draining on your own Spirit and Body at times, especially when you don't know when you'll be instructed to use it! Let me also warn you, this Gift is directly connected to your Emotions and that takes time to get used to, lol you have experienced it with me several times and not realizing that you were because many times those that God instructs you to use this Gift on, it will appear like they, will Soar without even a

Thank You. Then the Gift has settled down and you're left with your Emotions, but fortunately, you have me, and for years I had to Learn how to deal with this Awesome Gift alone.

My Response: Yes, I learned that this morning. I said to myself how can I touch someone else when someone in my household is suffering. But after God spoke I quickly had peace. In HIS time my family will be dealt with.

As for receiving a "thank you" or even seeing the fruits/testimony behind the "touch," I have NO desire to want to see what God does. I don't like to watch what I give (whether power or money) because I don't want to depend on seeing it! So I do what I'm supposed to do and keep it moving; God will do with it what he wants when he wants to; I did my part! Hopefully, this will help with the emotional part. I am grateful to have guidance; God will forever increase you for your obedience!

PC's Response: Yeah, Yeah, Yeah, lol. God chose me to deal with His Spoiled Child SMH but it has been a Joy seeing you Grow and Develop and there's even more! Just so you'll know, what God is doing is He's Equipping You, Building You, and

Strengthening You, all at the same time, for your Assignments! Each time you pour out it'll be a BURST, very draining!

My Response: YES!!!! Since this morning's encounter, I have been wearing my feelings on my sleeve—VERY sensitive—and the ONLY one who can trigger it is my husband. I'm being extremely patient with him in hopes that it shall pass.

PC's Response: Victor is going to trigger them lol. He's going to have you all over the place in your feelings lol; don't worry it'll pass but you must also be careful because the enemy will try to use him to get you all worked up but the one thing you've got going for you is Victor Truly Loves You and it hurts him to see you hurt! So he'll catch himself lol.

My Response: He has been catching himself but I still want to throat punch him and then pray for his healing lol.

A Handful of Prayers!!!

Vision #1 While at church singing and praising this is the vision I saw (**8:00 AM**): In church the angels and demons were present. They lined the ceiling all around the church as we sang the angels praised with wings spread, and the demons trembled. Down in the middle of the church right where my Pastor usually stands for alter calls, benedictions, and greetings were two Large arms reaching down from out of the sky (the ceiling was open in that spot), bright lights beamed down as we sung. The aroma of our praise (in the form of smoke) was collected by the large hands! SELAH! It gave me comfort to know I am seeded in good ground, and the heart of God looks down over my Pastor's flock!

Vision #2 (10:20 a.m.): During second service prayer time, as people gathered around the altar to pray, the two large hands were present as prayers were being sent up. I could see a grayish/black film coming off of the people (I gathered it was their cares, worries, infirmities, and issues) they were being collected by the hands. After this was finished, the hands rose up above the people facing down; now there was, "for lack of better terms," this light glittery gold dust flowing down onto the people; as I saw this in the spirit, I said to God, "Oh Lord please hear our prayers!" I felt confident that God was working on behalf of his people!

And when he had taken it, the four living creatures and the twenty-four elders fell down before the Lamb. Each one had a

143

harp and they were holding golden bowls full of incense, which are the prayers of God's people (**Revelation 5:8**).

Stop Clowning Around!

"The eye is the lamp of the body. If your eyes are healthy, your whole body will be full of light. But if your eyes are unhealthy, your whole body will be full of darkness. If then the light within you is darkness, how great is that darkness! (**Matthew 6:22, 23**).

Vision (4:57 a.m.): I saw a Clown Head sitting on top of a closed box. This is what the Lord said to me: **YOU DON'T HAVE TIME FOR FOOLISHNESS OR SILLY GAMES, STAY FOCUSED! KEEP YOUR MIND RIGHT. THE DEVIL IS LOOKING TO DISTRACT YOU WITH ALL KINDS OF TRICKERY; DO NOT ALLOW HIM IN. KEEP A LID ON YOUR MIND AND DO NOT ALLOW HIM IN! THERE IS SO MUCH I HAVE FOR YOU TO SEE....* At this time I was playing a lot of phone games, watching a lot of T.V., and interacting on social media—waking up to it and going to bed to it. God was desiring for me to spend time in his presence and I was preoccupied!

Stop Running!

Isaiah 41, 9b: *'You Are My Servant, I Have Chosen You and Have Not Cast You Away. 10 Fear Not, For I Am with You; Be Not Dismayed, For I Am Your God. I Will Strengthen You, Yes, I Will Help You, I Will Uphold You with My Righteous Right Hand.*

Journal Entry (6:00 a.m.): Right before I fully woke up this morning, I had a dream; there were two sets of hands. One set was much larger than the other set. The larger hands kept trying to wrap themselves around me and with the smaller hands I kept pulling them off of me. This happens several times and then I woke up. I quickly grabbed a pen and paper and this is what the Lord said to me: *WHY DO YOU KEEP FIGHTING ME? I WANT TO HOLD YOU, PROTECT YOU, LOVE YOU, AND GUIDE YOU WITH MY RIGHTEOUS HANDS.* (As I recorded, I saw a vision of him holding up nail-scarred hands.) He said: *LOOK AT MY HANDS, DO YOU KNOW WHAT POWER I HOLD; WHAT I HAVE DONE WITH THESE HANDS? COME TO ME AND LET ME CRADLE YOU. DO NOT FIGHT ME; DO NOT BE AFRAID, I DESIRE TO HOLD*

YOU AND TO KEEP YOU. APART FROM ME YOU CAN DO NOTHING BUT WITH ME; THERE IS NOTHING I WILL NOT DO FOR YOU! I WILL NOT FORCE YOU TO STAY IN MY ARMS, BUT I WILL URGE YOU THAT YOU DO NOT WANT TO BE WITHOUT ME. I LOVE YOU AND I WANT YOU TO REST IN MY ARMS.> I began to weep and I said to him, "I am sorry, Daddy; the closer I get to you the more I fear you and I don't know why. You are too awesome and too wonderful for me to be in your presence and even though you keep telling me to come to you, that I have nothing to fear, I still fear you. God, help me, I need your help!" He replied: *THERE IS SO MUCH THAT I WANT TO SHOW YOU; SO MUCH THAT I HAVE FOR YOU; IN MY VERY PRESENCE THERE IS HELP, PEACE, JOY, COMFORT, WISDOM, PROTECTION, AND MY POWER! I WANT TO GIVE IT ALL TO YOU BUT YOU HAVE TO STOP RUNNING FROM ME; YOU HAVE TO STOP PUSHING ME AWAY; THERE IS NOTHING TO FEAR! I LOVE YOU AND I AM FAITHFUL; THERE IS NOTHING YOU CAN DO TO LEAVE MY*

PRESENCE. WHEN YOU ARE READY, I WILL BE RIGHT HERE WAITING WITH OPEN ARMS.

*God pressed upon my heart to tell you to stop running! You may feel the same way that I feel; like you are not worthy, scared of what he may say to you, what he may show you, or what he may tell you to do, so you busy yourself to keep from hearing him, ignoring the tugging at your heart. God desires for you to STOP RUNNING. We cannot afford to go forward without him, to fight without him, or to make decisions without him; fear and pride can't help us; whatever it is that you are trying to do on your own, humble yourself and rest in his arms. He is willing, able and eagerly waiting to receive you. And when you're in his arms, there is NOTHING he will not do for you! **Luke 15:17-24**

The Gift of a Prayer Warrior!

Vision (8:15 a.m.): Yesterday during early morning church service it was prayer time, I closed my eyes to join in prayer and I was taken into the heavenly realm. I began to go higher and higher, and when I got to a certain level, I was blocked by a legion of Hell's demons. Standing before them I began to fear a little, then a multitude of God's angels flew in and began fighting them for me. As they fought an opening was created; I went through it and stood before a giant box. I climbed the box and began pulling out different gifts. I pulled out hope and threw it down to earth, faith, deliverance, healing; I began tossing them down one by one as I pulled them out of the box. I dug deeper and pulled out love; when I came across peace I held it tightly in my hands; I began to hug it and every angel fighting and every demon fighting back stood still frozen; I floated back down to earth past them all, carrying peace in my hands, then the vision stopped.

This is what the Lord said to me: *YOUR PRAYERS MUST BECOME DEEPER! I AM TAKING YOU TO ANOTHER REALM AND LEVEL IN WHICH I WILL RELEASE THROUGH YOU MY GIFTS. DO NOT FEAR OR WORRY ABOUT OPPOSITION; I WILL PROTECT YOU AND MAKE A WAY FOR YOU TO REACH ME! STAY IN PRAYER AND PRAY IN THE SPIRIT AT ALL TIMES AND IN EVERY WAY. MY GIFTS ARE COMING THROUGH THE PRAYERS I HAVE PLACED IN YOU!* (**Ephesians 6:10-18**)

I Got YOU!

Vision (6:32 a.m.): I see myself as a little girl holding Jesus' hand walking alongside him. But where He is walking the surface was smooth. I am climbing over rocks and a bumpy road. He is watching me intensely and holding my hand securely as I climb over each obstacle to make sure that I do not fall and that I make it over successfully. I don't have a care in the world, as I playfully climb and jump every step of the way, occasionally looking up at Him to see him smiling down at me. The scripture that dropped into my spirit was **Psalm 91**.

Take The Band-aid OFF!

6:00 a.m.: "Good Morning, Daddy!" I love you! song in my spirit (Holy; you must be holy. Holiness without which no man shall see; see the Lord).

Vision: I see myself walking with God as a child; I am skipping alongside Him. I stop, look down at my finger, and hold it up to Him with tears in my eyes; I say, "Daddy, I have a boo boo and it hurts." He grabs my hand and kisses my finger and immediately it heals. He says to me, *"SEE I FIXED IT"*! Then I hear the words, *"I DON'T DO BAND-AIDS"***Isaiah 53:5**

Then He said 6:15 a.m.: *MY LOVING CHILD, MY DESIRE FOR YOU IS TOTAL HEALING. YOU HAVE HAD TEMPORARY METHODS TO PATCH UP AND TO COVER UP THE WOUNDS IN YOUR LIFE. I NEED YOU TO SEEK ME FOR THIS. I KNOW IT HURTS; I KNOW THE PAIN YOU ARE FEELING; I KNOW THE PAIN MY SONS AND DAUGHTERS ARE HAVING. NONE OF WHICH CAN BE MENDED WITH BANDAGES. I DESIRE HOLINESS, I DESIRE HEALING, I DESIRE FULLNESS. COME TO ME WITH YOUR PAIN! COME TO ME WITH YOUR BROKENNESS, COME TO ME WITH YOUR SICKNESS, COME TO ME!* (**Matthew 11:28-30**).

Dream, Get Ready, Be Ready: I had a dream that I, my cousin, and someone else was going on a cruise. Prior to the date I kept saying I need to pack, I need to prepare for it; well the day came and although I was excited, I never got a chance to pack so I was throwing a few things into a bag to go. My cousin had told me we had to be on the boat by 6:30 p.m. so I took my time but by 5:35 p.m. I looked at the ticket and it said the boat LEAVES at 6:00 p.m.! Frantically I'm calling her to tell her she needs to get to the boat as fast as she can (she was driving so she could make it there in no time). I, however had to walk so I needed to run because I would barely make it in time. I was SO scared that I would miss the boat but I made it JUST in time; I could feel the panic leaving me until I realized I forgot my passport/documents needed to sail, then I woke up (**Matthew 25:1-13**). I KNEW what God was telling me: BE READY/GET PREPARED! As I was talking to the Lord this morning about what this meant for me, I began thinking of ways I believed I needed to prepare (read the word, not just devotional). God stopped my thoughts and said: *I AM THE WORD! SEEK ME! MY WORD IS ALREADY HIDDEN IN YOUR HEART. YOU DO NOT NEED TO SEARCH AND SEEK BOOK KNOWLEDGE; NOTHING CAN TELL YOU ABOUT ME OR YOU BETTER THAN MY LIVING RHEMA WORD! I HAVE GIVEN YOU THE GIFTING OF MY VOICE, VISION, DREAMS, PROPHECY, AND KNOWLEDGE, YOU CANNOT ACTIVATE OR FLOW IN IT WITHOUT ME!!! I AM THE VINE YOU ARE THE BRANCH; NO BRANCH CAN LIVE, GROW OR BE FRUITFUL WITHOUT THE VINE ...*

NO TREE CAN BARE FRUIT WITHOUT THE GARDENER'S TOUCH! (**John 15:1-8**) For me this means God desires me to just spend time in his presence, not watching T.V. ministries, not reading devotionals, not attempting to get "deep," and not just listening to gospel music but just sitting at his feet, listening to HIM speak! Glory to God; I've been so busy/lazy doing everything else and would say to myself, "If I can just read one scripture I will be fine or I would pray but wouldn't sit still long enough to listen." I will miss the boat doing this craziness! ARE YOU READY? (**Matthew 24:42-44**)

Dream, Feed My Sheep: I had a dream this morning. I gave birth to a baby boy. I was holding him and he was crying because he was hungry. I asked my daughter to go to the store to buy the baby some milk. She was taking her time to go, so the baby cried louder, he was looking up at me like he was starving. I yelled to my daughter, "HURRY UP, I NEED YOU TO GO AND GET HIS MILK, CAN'T YOU SEE HE IS HUNGRY AND CRYING." So she finally left to go to the store. While she was gone I had a thought to breastfeed him until she comes back. I began to breastfeed him and he was satisfied and stopped crying, then I woke up!

I asked the Lord what does this mean, He said to me: *"I HAVE ALREADY BIRTHED IN YOU WHAT IS NEEDED, WHY ARE YOU SEARCHING ELSEWHERE… IT'S ALREADY IN YOU"! FEED MY SHEEP"* (**John 21:15-17**).

Pour Out!

Luke 9: *When Jesus had called the Twelve together, he gave them power and authority to drive out all demons and to cure diseases, 2 and he sent them out to proclaim the kingdom of God and to heal the sick. 3 He told them: "Take nothing for the journey—no staff, no bag, no bread, no money, no extra shirt. 4 Whatever house you enter, stay there until you leave that town. 5 If people do not welcome you, leave their town and shake the dust off your feet as a testimony against them." 6 So they set out and went from village to village, proclaiming the good news and healing people everywhere.*

Vision (7:15 p.m.): While in church yesterday evening during a renewing service, I had a vision that there was no roof; looking down through the opening of the church was the Lord and a host of angels. As we sang the praise song, I begin to smile because I could see Him inhabiting and enjoying the praises being given up on his behalf; all while the angels partnered up and danced in circles. As service moved along it was prayer time; God intently listened to every heartbeat as we prayed; I began to pray for my Sister. He motioned several angels to go to her aide. Service went on as the visiting Pastor preached. His Sermon was Titled "Let It Flow." He preached from **2 Kings 4:1-7** (the widow with the small jar of olive oil) and he spoke about churches not tapping into the miraculous power we have available to us; the flowing power to heal, deliver, and set free, that we don't even have an expectation to see these things happen in our atmosphere or the faith to see God's glory flow. He hadn't even started preaching on his topic but this was confirmation for me. All I could think about was a conversation I had just a couple of days ago with my Sister about my desire to see God's glory in the church. I said to her, "I want to see people walk in sick and leave out healed, delivered, whatever their ailment is that God's people just begin to walk around touching each other, healing." (Paul's handkerchief and apron healed people **Acts 19:12**) I said, "There is NO reason why anyone within a church should still be walking around sick because Jesus said we would do greater works than he did!" (**John 14, 12**). *"Most assuredly, I say to you, he who believes in Me, the works that I do, he will do also, and greater works than these he will do, because I go to My Father. 13 And whatever you ask in My name, that I will do, that the Father may be glorified in the Son. 14 If you ask anything in My name, I will do it.* I then told her what God said to me. He said, *"STOP LOOKING TO SEE THESE THINGS HAPPEN AND EXPECT TO DO THEM"*! Moving toward the end of the Sermon which summed up to say use what you have and EXPECT God to increase you. As he ended with having everyone recite "Pour Out," I looked up and saw the Lord's finger pointing to me!

I AM WHO I AM!

Moses said to God, "Suppose I go to the Israelites and say to them, 'The God of your fathers has sent me to you', and they ask me, 'What is his name?' Then what shall I tell them?" God said to Moses, "I am who I am. This is what you are to say to the Israelites: 'I am has sent me to you'."God also said to Moses, "Say to the Israelites, 'The Lord, the God of your fathers—the God of Abraham, the God of Isaac, and the God of Jacob—has sent me to you'." "This is my name forever; the name you shall call me from generation to generation." **(Exodus 3:13-15)**.

Experience: On my drive into work this morning, the song "I Am" by Jason Nelson began to play and as I allowed the song to resonate in my spirit this is what the Lord said to me: *"I AM! TAKE THE LIMITS OFF OF ME; I HAVE NO LIMITS! I AM THE POSSIBLE TO THE IMPOSSIBLE. I AM ANYTHING AND EVERYTHING AND I AM EVERYWHERE; THERE ISN'T ANYWHERE THAT I HAVE NOT GONE ... EVEN TO THE CROSS! I AM WHO I AM, JUST LET ME BE WHO I AM TO YOU; I AM WHO I AM, JUST LET ME BE WHO I AM FOR YOU!"* >As I really sat back and meditated on those words, I began to shout and sing, healer, deliverer, power, protector, wealth, guidance, Savior, Alpha Omega Oh God, you will be there at the finish line just like you were there at my start (by then, I had no clue what the song was saying because I began to affirm what God is to me)! I began to realize the limits I've kept on God in my life; he is EVERYTHING TO ME! There is nothing he cannot do for or through me and I mean NOTHING! Wherever there is a lack in my life it's not because God can't or won't, it's my lack in faith that it can be done, not even thinking it possible. **Matthew 17:19, 20** says this: *Then the disciples came to Jesus in private and asked, "Why couldn't we drive it out?" He replied, "Because you have so little faith. Truly I tell you, if you have faith as small as a mustard seed, you can say to this mountain, 'Move from here to there,' and it will move. Nothing will be impossible for you."*

My focus is changing; it's not going to be on who or what he's already been and done but on what I have kept him from being and doing. Question 1. What/Who is He to you? 2. What have you kept Him from being and doing in your life? Now take the LIMITS OFF!!! (Ephesians 3:20).

Deer and Headlights!

Dream (2:30 a.m.): I was in my car with my kids and it stalled. As we sat there a deer ran out in front of us, it stopped and stared at the headlights. As it stood there, we watched as a spotted Tiger began prowling, peeking at it from the side of the car. I told the kids to watch what happens next. The Tiger jumped out and ambushed the deer and began to kill and eat it right there in front of us; we turned our heads not wanting to see the gory event. While the Tiger was distracted by eating the deer, I got out of the car popped the hood to see if I could get it started; I begin touching things, I had no clue what I was doing but when I told my son to turn the key in the ignition, the car started up! This caught the attention of the Tiger; I was scared stiff not knowing what the Tiger was about to do; that's when it ran over to me and began jumping on me, licking my hands, wanting me to pet him in approval for what he did. I was scared to death trying to understand what was happening, but I began petting him and gained confidence. With authority, I began telling him, "You are a good Tiger" and then the dream ended! When the alarm went off, for the first time in MONTHS I got up with ease, went to my threshing floor and was able to pray.

Deer: Distractions, stagnant, stalled, frozen, standing still. Tiger: Power, strength, aggression, fearless, leadership. This is what the Lord said to me: *ALL THAT HAS BEEN A DISTRACTION TO YOU I AM REMOVING! THIS SEASON WILL BE A SEASON OF PRODUCTIVITY; YOU WILL NO LONGER BE STAGNANT, STUCK IN A PLACE OF UNCERTAINTY. I WILL MAKE IT PLAIN TO YOU WHICH WAY TO GO; DO NOT FEAR; CHANGE IS GOOD, CHANGE IS COMING! YOU WILL CONQUEROR AND LEAD WITH AUTHORITY. ALL THAT CONCERNS YOU WILL BE DEALT WITH BY THE AUTHORITY I HAVE PLACED WITHIN YOU. DO NOT FEAR, THINK, OR WONDER. JUST MOVE WITH THE FLOW OF MY SPIRIT.*

Do not conform to the pattern of this world, but be transformed by the renewing of your mind. Then you will be able to test and approve what God's will is—his good, pleasing and perfect will (**Romans 12:2**).

Prior to the dream, I went to bed with some pressing issues on my mind and heart but when I woke up this morning, I felt a shifting. I finally believed in the power that God has placed within me, not because I earned it, learned it, or did anything to receive it. I have it simply because HE gave it to me! And now it's time to USE IT! I don't know how but I trust his spirit to show me what to do next. I will be entering this season not to take back the keys, but with the keys already in my hand, and with power and authority I will be releasing some things! NO FEAR and no distractions!!! Hallelujah!

On Other Ground Is Sinking Sand!

Dream: I was standing in a bedroom where the floor I was standing on turned to sand; each time the section that turned to sand caved in. I was fearful that I would fall through so I kept jumping to a different spot. I walked out of the room peeking into it, that's when the entire floor turned to sand and the whole room caved in and was destroyed.

The Scripture that came into my spirit: **Matthew 7:24-27**, 24 – "Therefore everyone who hears these words of mine and puts them into practice is like a wise man who built his house on the rock. 25 The rain came down, the streams rose, and the winds blew and beat against that house, yet it did not fall, because it had its foundation on the rock. 26 But everyone who hears these words of mine and does not put them into practice is like a foolish man who built his house on sand. 27 The rain came down, the streams rose, and the winds blew and beat against that house, and it fell with a great crash."

Favor "Ain't" Fair to a Screeching Rat!

Dream (5:15 a.m.): I had a dream that I kept hearing noises in the house but couldn't figure out what it was or where it was coming from. Then I saw this gray rat, it ran up and bit me in the foot. I was fearful and I chased it trying to smash it with a broom. I finally hit it and it screeched really loud; then I woke up.

I asked the Lord, "What does this mean?" He said to me: *THERE IS SOME SECRET CHATTER BEING SPOKEN AGAINST YOU. BUT YOU DO NOT HAVE TO DEFEND YOURSELF FOR I AM YOUR GOD AND WILL CORRECT ALL BEING SAID. DO NOT FEAR OR ALLOW THIS TO DISCOURAGE YOU. I AM YOUR GOD AND YOUR LOYALTY IS TO ME! YOU HAVE FOUND FAVOR IN MY SIGHT AND FAVOR IS NOT EARNED BUT GIVEN BY ME TO WHOM I CHOOSE. IF YOU HAVE FAVOR, THEN YOU*

WILL HAVE MY PEACE. YOU WILL BE SEATED AT THE TABLE OF PEACE ALONGSIDE THOSE THAT SPEAK AGAINST YOU, JUST AS I SAT AT THE TABLE WITH JUDAS. YOU WILL NOT HAVE TO DEFEND YOURSELF. THAT IS MY JOB TO DO FOR THOSE I FAVOR. STAY IN MY WILL AND MY FAVOR, PEACE, AND BLESSINGS WILL FLOW.

Luke 2:14: "Glory to God in the highest heaven, and on earth peace to those on whom his favor rests" (**Proverbs 16:28** and 1 **Chronicles 16:22**).

Transparency: I have ALWAYS feared what "man" thinks of me. As far back as I can remember, it has always been important for me to make sure I was seen as a good person even at the expense of hiding my talents and/or abilities and downplaying gifts in order for others to shine and feel good about themselves (AHAB!!!). But now God is stirring some things up in me that I HAVE to obey and with this, I am being approached to be placed in positions that put me on the front line. I want to be confident in what God has for me, continue to remain humble yet be effective. I do not want to be hindered because of seeking the loyalty and approval of "man." I have learned what God has for me it is for ME!!! So it CAN'T matter to me what people speak behind my back; favor ain't fair and it ain't mine to give back!

Black Butterfly!

Vision (5:48 p.m.): As I laid prostrate on the floor pouring out my heart to the Lord, I saw a Vision of a Black Butterfly flying erratically! This is what the Lord said to me: *I HAVE BROUGHT YOU OUT OF DARKNESS INTO THE MARVELOUS LIGHT. BUT BECAUSE YOU ARE SURROUNDED BY DARKNESS YOU CANNOT EFFECTIVELY FLY. I AM BRINGING YOU TO A PLACE OF LIGHT. PAY ATTENTION, MY DAUGHTER, AS I SHOW YOU STEP-BY-STEP WHAT I WILL COMMAND YOU TO DO; IT IS VITAL; MORE SO THAN EVER BEFORE! EVERYTHING I HAVE FOR YOU IS JUST BEYOND THE VEIL! THE DARKNESS WILL PROVOKE YOU TO DEPEND SOLELY ON FAITH IN ORDER TO POSSESS THAT WHICH IS NOT SEEN. MAKE NO MISTAKE. MY BLESSINGS AND MY PROMISES ARE REAL! I AM TAKING YOU TO THE*

OTHER SIDE OF BLESSED!> I said, "God, because you said it I believe you!" He replied: **THERE IS A TIME COMING WHERE I SHALL PLACE YOU BACK INTO A COCOON STATE; DO NOT FEAR, THIS IS TO SHIELD YOU FROM THAT WHICH I WILL BRING FORTH. NOTICE THAT IN THIS STATE YOU WILL BE UNABLE TO FUNCTION; THIS IS BECAUSE YOU WILL HAVE TO DO NOTHING AT THAT TIME. I WILL DO IT ALL; WHATEVER IS NEEDED, I WILL PROVIDE, AS I PREPARE YOU TO FLY. YOU WILL BE TOSSED BUT YOU WILL NOT BE HARMED. YOU WILL COME OUT STRONGER!* I got up and began to praise him and then I was prompted to lay back down.

6:15 p.m.: **AS YOU LAY ON THE THRESHING FLOOR, LAY IN THE FETAL POSITION, I WILL BE GOING ALL THE WAY BACK TO BIRTH; EVERY PLAN, EVERY SCHEME, EVERY EPISODE, EVERY SIN, EVERY EXPERIENCE UP UNTIL NOW I WILL FIX! EVERY CURSE PLACED ON YOUR LIFE WILL BE ABORTED!!! THUS SAITH THE LORD! I AM GOD; I CAN DO THIS AND I WILL DO THIS!* (Joel 2:20-32).

The Rebirthing!

Encounter (7:02 a.m.): As I lay on the threshing floor in the fetal position, I heard the word "REBIRTH"! Then the Lord said to me: **THERE IS A RE-BIRTHING TAKING PLACE IN YOU. I AM RESTORING EVERYTHING AND I MEAN EVERYTHING THAT WAS TAKEN FROM YOU; YOUR INNOCENCE, BLESSINGS, WISDOM, FINANCES, FAVOR, AND HONOR! THE CANKER WORM WILL REGURGITATE IT ALL! I LOVE YOU, MY DAUGHTER, AND YOU HAVE FOUND FAVOR IN MY SIGHT.>* Daddy, show me your glory (Ezekiel 1:25-28, Joel 2:23-28)

Cocoon State!

I had a vision of a cocoon that was being tossed around, and this is what the Lord said to me: "*I HAVE SEPARATED YOU AND COVERED YOU AND WILL PROTECT YOU EVEN IN THE SHAKING PROCESS. DO NOT WORRY OR FEAR.*" At that time, I had been going through in my marriage, my own personal mind, and space. After I got through that process I saw another vision. I saw a caterpillar come out of the cocoon and turn into a butterfly. It was beautiful, VERY colorful but when I looked out beyond the land as far as I could see everything was completely gray. I opened my mouth to sing and the butterfly began to fly and everything it touched began to display rich, deep colors until the entire scene was colorful. The Lord said to me: *"I WILL USE YOU TO TOUCH THE WORLD"*.

His Voice, I Am in AWE of You!

Exercise: Meditate and think about something that fills you in AWE of God!

I began thinking on the colors of fish, the process of plants, the ocean.

Journal (12:21 p.m.): God, you are glorious, marvelous, creative, colorful, powerful, BIG, wide, intelligent, emotional, caring, a judge, in everything, spontaneous, surprising, unlimited, high yet you look low, ever-changing yet the same, I am in AWE of you!!!

His Response: *MY DAUGHTER I LOVE YOU AND I MADE YOU OUT OF ALL THAT YOU SEE IN ME! YOU ARE UNIQUE, CREATIVE, COLORFUL, POWERFUL, LOVING, CARING; YOU ARE A REFLECTION OF ME AND I AM*

PROUD TO CALL YOU MY DAUGHTER. WHEN I MADE YOU I THOUGHT CAREFULLY OF HOW I WOULD KNIT YOU TOGETHER, WHO YOU WOULD LOOK LIKE, YOUR SMILE, YOUR WAYS, YOUR DAYS. WHAT TRIALS YOU WOULD FACE, HOW I WOULD HELP YOU OVERCOME THEM AND THE POWER AND TESTIMONY THAT WOULD BE DEVELOPED FROM THOSE TRIALS. I LOVE YOU AND I HAVE BEEN IN AWE OF YOU SINCE THE DAY OF CREATION! (Psalm 139)

Walk in Your Freedom!

Dream (5:15 a.m.): I had a dream that I pulled two dead parasites out of my left ear, the only thing left was their bones. They were snake-like.

Prayer: Daddy, I love you and I bless you please tell me what this means? *I LOVE YOU MY DAUGHTER AND FIRST I MUST DEAL WITH YOUR SPIRIT WITHIN; YOU ARE NOT TRUSTING ME! I HAVE GIVEN YOU PROMISES THAT WILL COME TO PASS AND I HAVE GIVEN YOU THE POWER TO FIGHT! YOU MUST USE MY WORD AGAINST ALL THAT COMES UP AGAINST YOU. I AM NOT TALKING*

ABOUT YOUR HUSBAND; I AM TALKING ABOUT THE LYING SPIRITS YOU ALLOW YOURSELF TO LISTEN TO. SHAME AND CONDEMNATION! STOP ALLOWING YOURSELF TO LIVE IN YOUR PAST, I HAVE CREATED YOU NEW. EVERYTHING I HAVE TO GIVE TO YOU IS NEW. DO NOT LET THE ENEMY TRICK YOU INTO BELIEVING THAT I AM NOT MORE POWERFUL OR STRONGER THAN YOUR CIRCUMSTANCE. IT IS NOT HOPELESS, YOUR SITUATION IS NOT HOPELESS. REST IN ME! YOU KNOW ME, MY DAUGHTER, I HAVE NEVER LEFT YOU NOR WILL I FORSAKE YOU. I AM ALWAYS HERE WAITING AND WATCHING YOU. SEEK ME ESPECIALLY WHEN YOU ARE GOING THROUGH; FIGHT, MY DAUGHTER, FIGHT! I HAVE RELEASED YOU FROM YOUR PAST; WALK IN YOUR FREEDOM AND DO NOT BE ENTANGLED BY THE LIES! **(2 Corinthians 5:17)**

Chapter XII: Conversations with God!

Throughout this book, God made it very clear; stay focus, stay at his feet, pray, seek his presence and listen for his voice! I cannot express to you how many times I have either survived my own attacks, survived other people's attacks and/or survived the attacks of the enemy just by talking to the Father and listening to what he had to say to me. This chapter consists of dialog with God! I pray that as you read these conversations that you will see yourself on these pages and hear God speaking directly to YOU!

Take the Limits OFF! *"TAKE THE LIMITS OFF! RELEASE ME! YOU LACK THE CONFIDENCE OF THE POWER I'VE ALREADY PLACED WITHIN YOU, SO YOU WALK AROUND IN MEEKNESS, SHYNESS, AND TIMIDITY SAYING THINGS AT JUST AN EARSHOT AWAY. BUT I HAVE CREATED YOU TO SHOUT FROM THE MOUNTAIN. WHAT I HAVE PLACED IN YOU THE WORLD NEEDS TO HEAR; NOT JUST WHO YOU FEEL COMFORTABLE SAYING IT IN FRONT OF. I NEED YOU TO BE BOLD! WHAT I HAVE TO SAY THROUGH YOU IS MORE IMPORTANT THAN*

"FEELINGS" I WILL NOT ALWAYS USE YOU THROUGH AN EMAIL, TEXT, OR BOOKS. I WANT YOU FRONT AND CENTER!" (**2Timothy 1:7**).

Follow Me! *I LOVE YOU, MY DAUGHTER; DO YOU NOT TRUST ME TO SAVE YOU FROM ANY AND ALL THAT CAN HARM YOU? I WILL NOT ALWAYS PROVIDE A WAY OUT; SOME THINGS WILL REQUIRE YOU TO LET GO AND TRUST ME! I AM THE WAY, THE TRUTH, AND THE LIFE; FOLLOW ME!*

Let It FLOW! (1:15 p.m.): Sitting in Stone Mountain Park by the lake, I began writing in my journal. I love you, Daddy, and I am so glad to be here with you alone! He said: *I LOVE YOU, MY DAUGHTER, AND I AM GLAD TO HAVE YOU ALL TO MYSELF. DO YOU SEE THIS WATER FLOWING; THE PATTERN IN WHICH IT FLOWS EASY, STEADY, AND ALL TOGETHER? THIS IS WHAT I DESIRE WITH YOU; I DESIRE FOR MY SPIRIT TO FLOW WITHOUT HINDRANCE; STEADY TOGETHER USING ALL THE SPIRITUAL GIFTS I HAVE GIVEN YOU. *YOU WANT TO KNOW ABOUT YOUR DREAMS? THEY ALL WORK TOGETHER AND WILL COME*

TO PASS, STAY CLOSE TO ME AND I WILL REVEAL THEM TO YOU. Looking at the fall trees across the lake, the three different shades of yellow, orange and brown, I said, "Daddy, your world has so much beauty in it." He interrupted me and said, "*YOU ARE BEAUTIFUL, MY DAUGHTER, INSIDE AND OUT AND YES YOUR HUSBAND WILL CALL YOU BLESSED; YOUR CHILDREN WILL CALL YOU BLESSED BECAUSE I HAVE BLESSED YOU AND I WILL CONTINUE TO REVEAL MY BLESSINGS IN YOU AND THROUGH YOU. YOU ARE BLESSED! WALK IN IT, DO NOT FEAR MY BLESSINGS. I WILL USE THEM TO BLESS OTHERS; THEY WILL FLOW STEADY JUST AS YOU SEE THE WATER FLOW.*" (I have recently been fascinated with Mahilia Jackson's music and I purchased her CD; I have been absorbing her music to the point whereas I listen and just cry; it does something to me). I asked God, "Why Mahilia Jackson?" He said: *BECAUSE HER SOUL WAS PURE; HER MUSIC REFLECTS EVERYTHING WITHIN THAT IS PURE. YOU, MY DAUGHTER, ARE BEING MADE WHOLE; HER MUSIC TOUCHES YOU; WHICH MEANS YOU HAVE A DESIRE*

FOR PURE THINGS. THIS IS WHAT I CAN USE; I AM USING AND WILL USE EVERYTHING I HAVE PLACED IN YOU. YOU FIRST HAVE TO GO TO FULL TERM AND THEN THERE WILL BE LABOR PAINS BUT DO NOT FEAR; WHAT WILL COME AFTERWARD IS DELIVERANCE, HEALING, AND POWER. YOU WILL FORGET ALL FORMER PAIN AND WILL COMPLETELY FOCUS ON WHAT I HAVE BIRTHED THROUGH YOU. I WILL PROTECT YOU THROUGH THIS ENTIRE PROCESS. MY DAUGHTER IF ONLY YOU COULD HANDLE THE THINGS I AM DOING THROUGH YOU. SOON YOU WILL BE ABLE TO HANDLE IT ALL. GREATER THINGS, GREATER THINGS, GREATER THINGS THEN THESE ... YE SHALL DO! The scriptures that came into my spirit were **John 16:21** And **John 14:12**.

WHY God??? Journal Entry (7:15 a.m.): I woke up this morning praying; I said, "God bless this person, protect that person, thank you for this, and thank you for that." But this and that wasn't really on my heart. I stopped and I said, "God, I have fear in my heart and I know this is not from you. I trust you and I know that you are a compassionate God and not an evil God but why do bad things happen to good people and why do you allow it? (*Real talk*)." God said to me: *I DO NOT STAND AT THE DOOR OPENING IT FOR GOOD AND EVIL; I KNOW THE END FROM THE BEGINNING AND I SET THE WORLD UP FROM THE BEGINNING TO THE END. I SEE THE THINGS THAT YOU DO NOT SEE; THINGS THAT I KNOW WILL BRING ME GREATER GLORY, THINGS THAT WILL DEVELOP HEALING, THINGS THAT WILL STRENGTHEN FAITH, AND THINGS THAT WILL SAVE SOULS. I AM THE ANSWER!* (**Romans 8:28**)

I'm Tired! Journal Entry (9:05 a.m.): Lord, sometimes I get tired of praying until I don't know what to pray for anymore! He said: *DO NOT GET WEARY IN WELL DOING; YOU WILL GET TO SEE MY GLORY IF YOU FAINT NOT! MY SPIRIT WILL HELP YOU IN WAYS YOU CANNOT EVEN IMAGINE... REST! COME TO ME AND REST! DO NOT LET LIFE BE A DISTRACTION TO YOU; I HAVE ALREADY OVERCOME ANYTHING YOU COULD GO THROUGH. REJOICE IN THE VICTORY EVEN IF YOU CANNOT SEE IT*

WITH YOUR NATURAL EYES; SEE IT WITH YOUR SPIRITUAL EYES. I AM IN EVERY SITUATION WORKING BEHIND THE SCENE. PRAISE ME FOR MY WONDROUS WORKS! (I started praising but my mind began to drift.) He said it again: *REST!* (**Romans 8:26, 27**).

Press! *I LOVE YOU, MY DAUGHTER, AND I AM GLAD THAT YOU CHOSE TO PRESS! ALWAYS REMEMBER I WILL NOT FORCE YOU INTO THIS PLACE. YOU MUST DESIRE TO BE HERE AND THEN FIGHT YOUR WAY THROUGH. SATAN WILL NEVER MAKE IT EASY, YOUR FLESH WILL NOT MAKE IT DESIRABLE BUT YOUR SPIRIT IS ALWAYS WILLING! YOU MUST COME TO ME IN SPIRIT AND IN TRUTH. THIS IS WHERE I WILL ALWAYS BE, I WILL NEVER LEAVE YOU. THERE IS SO MUCH MORE THAT I HAVE FOR YOU AND IT IS ONLY THROUGH YOUR WILLINGNESS AND OBEDIENCE THAT I WILL BE ABLE TO TAKE YOU THERE. RISE UP! SET A NEW STANDARD FOR YOURSELF. COME TO ME AND FIGHT THE GOOD FIGHT OF FAITH. I LOVE YOU, MY CHILD.* (**Philippians 3:14**)

Smoke Screen! As I laid prostrate before the Lord, pouring out the issues that flowed from my heart, I felt myself being attacked by condemnation, self-pity, regret for past hurts and choices, could-haves, should-haves. God interrupted these thoughts and said two words to me, *"SMOKE SCREEN"*! I took a deep breath, blew out in a sigh really hard and the fog began to fade away. That's when I could clearly see the promises God made to me! *Some things are designed to cloud our vision, blind our hope but God asks us to *BREATHE!* It's only a Smoke Screen....

Daily Bread! 7:20 a.m.: Good Morning, God, I love you! I bless your holy name; Daddy, I NEED you; at this time I felt drained I had not been sitting still long enough to hear God speak!!! He said to me: *DAUGHTER, YOU HAVE ME! I HAVE NEVER LEFT YOU, YOU MUST COME INTO MY PRESENCE DAILY IN ORDER TO RECEIVE WHAT I HAVE FOR YOU. YOU CANNOT LIVE OFF OF YESTERDAY'S BREAD. YOU MUST COME TO ME TO RECEIVE WHAT ONLY I CAN GIVE YOU. NOT YOUR HUSBAND,*

CHILDREN, JOB BUT ONLY I CAN GIVE IT TO YOU. SUP WITH ME AND I WILL FILL YOU UP TO OVERFLOW!

STAY FOCUSED! I said to Him, "Daddy, please forgive me for forsaking you, for turning away from you, for not listening and not seeking your presence. I need you!" He replied: **SET THE ATMOSPHERE EVERYWHERE YOU GO! THE DAYS OF SITTING BACK AND WATCHING ARE OVER! I HAVE COMMANDED MUCH OF YOU. STAY FOCUSED, STAY FOCUSED, STAY FOCUSED! STAY IN MY PRESENCE. YOU WILL NOT BE ABLE TO MOVE UNTIL YOU PAY ATTENTION TO WHAT I WILL SHOW YOU. THE TIME IS NOW! NO MORE PLAYING GAMES! IT IS TIME TO GET SERIOUS. I FORGIVE YOU MY DAUGHTER BUT YOU MUST PAY ATTENTION TO MY STILL SMALL VOICE. YOU WILL MISS IT IF YOU SWAY TO THE LEFT OR THE RIGHT. I NEED YOU TO DO MY WILL.* (**Matthew 4:4**)

You Love Me through my Good and Bad! Daddy, thank you for waking me up this morning; speak to me, Lord! I ask you for the forgiveness of my sins; my attitude, my heart, my anger, my speech, my pride, etc. Help me to do better and be better!

MY DAUGHTER, I LOVE YOU THROUGH YOUR GOOD AND YOUR BAD; YOU MUST LEARN TO LOVE OTHERS THROUGH THEIR GOOD TIMES AND BAD TIMES; IT MUST NOT ONLY BE IN WORDS BUT IT MUST BE IN YOUR HEART AND IN YOUR ACTIONS. THIS WILL HELP TO HEAL THEM FROM THEIR PAST. YOU PLANT, I WATER AND MAKE GROW. BE PATIENT, KIND IN ALL THAT YOU DO; THIS IS MY LOVE ... THIS IS HOW MY LOVE FLOWS, PATIENTLY, KIND, FAITHFUL, PROTECTIVE—READ MY WORD ON LOVE. But, Daddy, I've tried to do this and it's not coming back to me; I don't get the same in return! *MY DAUGHTER, NEITHER DO I NOT EVEN FROM YOU! BUT I STILL LOVE YOU WITH EVERY FIBER OF MY BEING AND I STILL FORGIVE YOU AND SHOW YOU. DO NOT ALLOW OTHERS TO TAKE YOU OUTSIDE OF THE BOUNDARIES OF MY LOVE. THEIR HEALING DEPENDS ON YOU GETTING THIS RIGHT; YOU DO THIS FOR THEM AND WATCH WHAT I DO FOR YOU!*

(1Corinthians 13:4-7)

The Heart! Vision (7:05 a.m.): Lord, I see a giant hand holding a heart covered in blood; What are you trying to say to me? God replied: *I HAVE THE HEART OF MAN IN MY HAND. I KNOW ABOUT EVERYTHING, MY BLOOD COVERS THE LOVE THAT PUMPS THROUGH YOUR HEART! LOVE PASSIONATELY, LOVE WHOLEHEARTEDLY, LOVE UNCONDITIONALLY. I AM READY TO TEACH YOU HOW BUT YOU MUST SUBMIT YOUR HEART TO ME SO THAT I AM NOT FIGHTING AGAINST YOU. I DESIRE YOU TO BE A WILLING VESSEL IN THE PALM OF MY HANDS SO THAT I AM ABLE TO SHAPE YOUR HEART INTO ANYTHING I CHOOSE TO! STAY OPEN AND STAY CLOSE TO ME.* **(Psalm 51:10)**

The Battle Is the Lords! Vision (6:05 a.m.): God, I see a man on a horse galloping off into the sunset. I heard the word BATTLEFIELD! Now I see several horses and men riding on them; as they are riding a giant hand is picking them up one by one. Daddy, what does this mean? He said to me: *THE BATTLE IS MINE! SOME BATTLES YOU WILL NEED TO FIGHT, SOME BATTLE YOU WILL NOT; I PICK AND*

CHOOSE! IT IS UP TO YOU TO BE IN TUNE WITH MY SPIRIT IN ORDER FOR YOU TO KNOW WHICH ONES I HAVE DESIGNED FOR YOU TO FIGHT IN ORDER FOR YOU TO GROW AND WHICH ONES I AM FIGHTING IN ORDER TO SHOW YOU MY GLORY! LEARN FROM ME, TAKE MY YOKE UPON YOU, AND LEARN FROM ME! **(Exodus 14:14)**

War in the Heavenly! Daddy, I pray that you help me stay in tune with your spirit so that I may know when to fight and when to stand down. Teach me your wisdom. God, when I do need to fight, help me to use my Spiritual weapons and armor you speak of in **Ephesians 6**. He replied: **I LOVE YOU, MY CHILD, AND I HAVE SPECIAL PLANS FOR YOU. KEEP SUPPING WITH ME, KEEP COMING TO THE TABLE. YOU WILL GAIN STRENGTH TO FIGHT ALL BATTLES, EVEN ONES THAT ARE NOT YOURS. THERE IS A SPIRITUAL WAR GOING ON AND I AM EQUIPPING YOU IN ORDER THAT YOU MAY SEE IT AND NOT FEAR WHAT YOU SEE. YOU ARE MY SPECIAL CHOSEN GEM. I LOVE YOU.*

Vision (6:25 a.m.): I see a man on a horse with a sword in his hand. *AS YOU SUP WITH ME YOU WILL BEGIN TO DEVELOP EVERY WEAPON THAT IS NEEDED NOT TO WIN THIS BATTLE BUT TO FIGHT IT; I ALREADY WON THE WAR. THE SWORD, WHICH IS MY WORD IS THE MOST IMPORTANT WEAPON OF THEM ALL! LEARN OF ME!* (**Matthew 11:29**)

I Told the Storm! As I was praying and praising the song, I Told the Storm dropped into my spirit - *Even though your winds blow I want you to know. You cause me no alarm cause I'm safe in His arms. Even though your rain falls I can still make this call; let there be peace. Now I can say go away....*

Vision (6:58 a.m.): As I heard the song, the entire atmosphere around me turned gray, rainy, and stormy. I began to sing out loud with all my might as I pointed and the words came out of my mouth, everything around me began to display color. I was commanding PEACE! God said to me: **MY DAUGHTER, THIS IS WHAT I WANTED YOU TO SEE; THIS IS WHAT I WILL DO THROUGH YOU. YOU NEVER HAVE TO FEAR BECAUSE IT IS BY MY POWER AND MIGHT THAT THIS*

WILL BE DONE! I WILL GIVE YOU THE AUTHORITY TO COMMAND THE STORM TO CONTROL THE WINDS OF LIFE. YOU ARE MY CHOSEN ONE. I LOVE YOU; ALL I NEED IS A WILLING VESSEL TO FLOW FREELY THROUGH. THIS IS WHY I NEED YOU AT A PLACE THAT IS FREE OF HINDRANCE; A PLACE OF PEACE! (**Isaiah 26:3**)

The Waltz! Daddy, I am pressing into your presence to behold the beauty of your face!

Vision (6:23 a.m.): I see myself in a ballroom gown; dancing with you face to face. (I almost feel like I'm at a Father/Daughter Dance). "Daddy, I feel like a princess, dancing with a King!" He replied: *YOU ARE MY LITTLE PRINCESS*! I see a group of homeless people standing by the door waiting for it to open up. What does this mean? He said: *YOU WILL FEED MY LOST. MAN CANNOT LIVE BY BREAD ALONE BUT BY EVERY WORD THAT PROCEEDS OUT OF MY MOUTH! YOU WILL SEE A PHYSICAL DIFFERENCE IN THOSE WHO KNOW ME AND THOSE WHO DO NOT. THEY WILL LOOK LOST, HOMELESS, AND*

DEPRIVED IN YOUR EYES. I WILL NEED YOU TO FEED THEM. DO NOT WORRY ABOUT WHAT YOU SHALL SAY OR DO IN THAT HOUR; I WILL FLOW THROUGH YOU! IT WILL BE LIKE A DANCE; WE WILL FLOW TOGETHER, IN SINC, LIKE A WALTZ ... 1, 2, 3, 1, 2,3. MY GLORY WILL BE REVEALED. KEEP FOCUSED ON ME AND I WILL DO THE REST! (**John 15:4**)

Tattletale! Vision: I see myself as a child and I am standing with other children. I am pointing out their faults!"Ooh, Daddy, see, look what he is doing; look what she is doing"! This is what the Lord said: **DO NOT POINT OUT SOMEONE ELSE' SPECK AND NOT TAKE CARE OF YOUR OWN ISSUES. I AM GOD AND I CAN SEE ALL THINGS. THIS IS NOT THE TIME TO EXAMINE OTHERS; THIS IS A TIME TO EXAMINE YOURSELF! SO THAT YOU MAY BE ABLE TO SEE THEM AND YOURSELF AS I SEE YOU THROUGH FORGIVING EYES, THROUGH COMPASSIONATE EYES, THROUGH MERCIFUL EYES.*

Prayer (6:22 a.m.): Daddy, forgive me where I have found fault in others; help me to focus on repenting for my own sinful deeds, that I may be blameless in your sight! (**Matthew 7:1**)

Sand as far as the Eyes Could See! Vision (1:22 p.m.): I see myself as a child with my chin resting on my hands as I gazed at my Heavenly Father. He stretches out his hand and presents what he wants me to see. Open space full of sand as far as the eyes could see. He begins showing me something but I didn't see anything but sand. *THIS IS YOUR TESTIMONY; YOU SHALL SHARE IT WITH THE WORLD. AS FAR AS THE SANDS YOU SEE, I WILL ALLOW YOUR VOICE TO TRAVEL. YOU ARE MY MOUTHPIECE, YOU ARE A REPRESENTATION OF ME. WHAT I SAY YOU WILL SAY; WHAT I SEE YOU SHALL SEE. YOU WILL REACH THE MULTITUDES.* (**Psalm 139:17-18**)

Spirit Willing! I woke up this morning praying about spiritual growth and thanking God for not leaving me and allowing my spirit man to get its act together. God quickly corrected me: *THE SPIRIT IS ALWAYS WILLING; IT IS WHEN YOU ALLOW YOUR FLESH TO GROW STRONGER THAT IT*

RULES OVER YOU. THE SPIRIT NEVER DENIES TRUTH, ALWAYS FOLLOWS INSTRUCTION AND ALWAYS HAS THE ANSWERS. THE SPIRIT WITHIN YOU IS ME AND I CANNOT FAIL! ONE MUST PUT TO DEATH DAILY THE FLESH SO THAT THE SPIRIT MAY HAVE FULL REIGN! **(Mark 14:38)**.

Face Your Fears! Dream: I had a dream that I was out of town and was trying to get home. As I was making my way home, there were several different obstacles in my way. One of which was: I was on an extremely tall roof trying to climb my way down but the way down was hard and scary! I was with other people but I was in the front so I had to go first, which meant I did not have anyone that I could mimic the pattern of how to get down. There were several ladders but you had to slide down a pole first in order to reach the level of the ladders. My fear was if I started to slide down I would not be able to stop when I reached the bottom and I would severely hurt myself once I landed or I would slip off the pole and fall to my death! I stood there with the group agonizing over this to the point of tears. I did not want to do it! Finally, I noticed that

184

there were levers on the poles that I could hold on and jump down each level until I made contact with the ladders! So that's what I did…. When I reached the bottom I felt so much relief! When I looked back up the ladder, my earthly father was standing on the last level before the ground cheering me on! I heard the words *"FACE YOUR FEARS!"* *DIANE MY CHILD YOU HAVE NOTHING TO FEAR I AM WITH YOU ALWAYS. IF YOU SEEK ME WITH YOUR WHOLE HEART I AM ALWAYS AVAILABLE TO YOU. I HAVE NOT GIVEN YOU THE SPIRIT OF FEAR BUT A SOUND MIND TO MAKE SOUND DECISIONS. FACE YOUR CHALLENGES; YOU WILL SUCCEED! DO NOT FEAR I AM WITH YOU ALWAYS. TAKE CAREFUL STEPS IN ALL THAT YOU DO AND AVOID SLIDING DOWN THE PITFALLS OF THIS LIFE; INCLUDE ME IN EVERYTHING THAT YOU DO; IT WILL HELP YOU AVOID FALLING INTO TEMPTATION. I ALWAYS GIVE YOU A WAY OUT. I AM THE WAY THE TRUTH AND THE LIFE; COME TO ME! TAKE COURAGE MY DAUGHTER AND BE BRAVE. I HAVE GIVEN YOU EVERYTHING YOU NEED TO SUCCEED. I AM VERY PROUD OF YOU.*

Don't Eat the Fruit! (6:00 a.m.): I heard Satan whisper to me, *"there is no power in Jesus' name; Jesus doesn't have any power. it is God who has the power; eat the fruit and you will be like God!"* Then the Lord spoke to me: **TEMPTATION IS COMING, BUT I HAVE GIVEN YOU EVERYTHING YOU NEED TO RESIST THE DEVIL. I HAVE GIVEN YOU A WAY OUT. IT WILL NOT BE I WHO TEMPTS YOU NOR WILL IT BE A TEST FROM ME, IT IS THE FLESH AND ITS DESIRES THAT WILL COME AGAINST YOU. YOU MUST REMAIN IN MY SPIRIT! WATCH OUT AND PAY ATTENTION JUST LIKE WITH EVE IT WILL LOOK DESIRABLE; IT WILL LEAD TO DEATH IN YOUR SPIRIT. I AM WITH YOU ALWAYS!* **(James 1:13-15) Vision (6:15 a.m.):** I see this shapely woman standing underneath a giant creepy hand. I heard the words "Spirit of Seduction." Daddy, what does this mean? *THE SPIRIT OF SEDUCTION WILL TRY YOU. STAND YOUR GROUND; I AM THE RIGHT HAND OF RIGHTEOUSNESS AND I WILL PROTECT YOU IF YOU LET ME. DO NOT ALLOW YOURSELF TO BE SEDUCED BY EVIL THOUGHTS OR WAYS. IT WILL COME IN MANY*

186

FORMS, YOU MUST STAY HOLY FOR I AM HOLY. CONTINUE TO PRAY, CONTINUE TO SEEK ME WITH YOUR WHOLE HEART; I AM ALWAYS HERE FOR YOU. I AM ALWAYS WITH YOU. DO NOT FEAR MY PRESENCE. STAY CLOSE TO THE VINE (**1Peter 1:16**).

You Are Beautiful! *6:45 AM* This morning I was able to do my normal routine in my room (Victor was not home). I put anointing oil on my hands and I usually anoint myself from head to toe. But this morning God had me to kneel before him (He was going to do it!). I knelt at the edge of my bed with my hands up singing "you are welcome in this place!" (My temple). As I closed my eyes I was before the throne kneeling. Jesus stood in front of me with his hands on my head. I begin speaking in tongues as I touched my own head in the natural; God Spoke: (He touched every area in the spirit as I touched in the natural; I spoke in tongues and he translated what was said in English and I spoke it out loud)

AS I TOUCH YOUR HEAD I AM GIVING YOU MY THOUGHTS; EVERYTHING I NEED YOU TO KNOW YOU

WILL KNOW.   NO MORE DOUBT; NO MORE DISTRACTIONS I AM REMOVING THEM!

EYES; *I WILL INCREASE YOUR VISION; I WILL SHOW YOU THINGS BEYOND YOUR OWN PERIPHERAL.   YOU WILL SEE THINGS IN OTHERS IN ORDER TO HELP THEM AND GIVE THEM EXACTLY WHAT I GIVE TO YOU FOR THEM.*

EARS; *I AM OPENING YOUR EARS!* (my left ear has been feeling clogged lately, he touched my ears and yanked away from my head as to release something; I could hear clearly!) *YOUR HEARING WILL BE PRECISE, YOU WILL NO LONGER HEAR FROM THE OTHER VOICES.   YOU WILL ONLY HEAR FROM ME! YOU MUST TRUST THAT IT IS ME SPEAKING TO YOU DIANE; I WILL GIVE YOU MY SECRETS! I AM OPENING MY WORLD TO YOU!*

MOUTH; *YOU WILL SPEAK WITH BOLDNESS, WITH ACCURACY, THUS SAITH THE LORD; WITH TENDERNESS, LOVE, GRACE.   DO NOT ALLOW YOURSELF TO SPEAK ILL INTENT OF OTHERS. GIVE ME YOUR CARES, NO*

MORE COMPLAINING; I HEAR EVERYTHING! (I asked forgiveness for my recent complaining that I knew God was speaking on!)

THROAT; *YOUR VOICE HAS GROWN AND MATURED. I AM TOUCHING YOUR NATURAL WITH MY SUPERNATURAL. NO MORE DOUBT; TRAIN YOUR EARS TO HEAR WHAT I HEAR. THE BEAUTY IN YOUR IMPERFECTIONS; THE BEAUTY IN YOUR SINCERITY AND IN YOUR WORSHIP! IT IS PURE!!*

HEART; *YOUR HEART BEATS FOR ME; I HAVE IT IN THE PALM OF MY HAND; KEEP IT THERE! YOU ARE A WOMAN AFTER MY OWN HEART! I AM WELL PLEASED....*

STOMACH; *STAY SENSITIVE TO MY SPIRIT AS HE GUIDES YOU. IT IS ME GUIDING YOU BECAUSE I AM IN YOU. YOU WILL KNOW HOW TO MOVE.*

FEET; *CONTINUE TO WALK IN MY WAYS AND YOU WILL WALK ON WATER! THIS IS A METAPHOR.... WALKING ON WATER INDICATES THE LEVEL OF TRUST YOU HAVE IN ME AND THE LEVEL OF TRUST I HAVE IN YOU TO BID*

YOU TO COME! KEEP YOUR EYES ON ME AND EVERYTHING I HAVE TOLD YOU WILL COME TO PASS.

I begin to weep! He then led me in the spirit to sit on his right side of the throne. I rested my feet on top of this "thing" that knelt trembling; this is what the Lord said:

*EVERY ENTITY ASSIGNED TO YOUR LIFE WILL BECOME YOUR FOOTSTOOL! EVERY PERSON SPEAKING AGAINST YOU; THE SECRET CHATTER... EVERY PERSON SECRETLY HARBORING JEALOUSY, ENVY, CAUSING STRIFE BEHIND YOUR BACK (I began to think because I have NO clue who they are) *WILL BE SITTING AT THE TABLE I AM PREPARING FOR YOU. THEY WILL WATCH AS I GIVE THEIR PLATES TO YOU! THE WEALTH OF THE WICKED IS BEING STORED UP FOR YOU!!! THUS SAITH THE LORD! I AM WELL PLEASED IN YOU MY DAUGHTER!*

I cried out who am I Daddy? I am no different.... he interrupted me. *YOU ARE DIFFERENT; I MADE YOU DIFFERENT! GET THAT IN YOUR SPIRIT!* I said OK Daddy, I AM different! Please keep me humble.....*YOU ALREADY ARE....*

BECAUSE I AM!

.........AND YOU ARE BEAUTIFUL!!!

Conclusion

Walking by faith is crossing the bridges of life uncertain of what lies at the other end yet still moving, still living, still seeking His presence. God desires to show YOU what's behind the veil!!!

As I sum up my journey I am entering into the manifestations of all that God has spoken; every promise, every vision, every conversation, every lesson learned, and every detail spoken…. I AM WALKING IN IT! I can't even express what I am feeling at this moment as I finalize what I am writing to you. Everything that God has spoken is ATTAINABLE. I know this and I believe it is so!!! But the good news is he does not just speak to ME, he speaks to ALL of his children if we learn to listen. The word says in **John 10:27**, *My sheep hear My voice, and I know them, and they follow Me.* There is not a person connected to God that cannot hear him speak… LISTEN TO HIM; OPEN UP YOUR HEART TO RECEIVE HIS WORD SPECIFIC AND TAILORED JUST FOR YOU! There is a world he is waiting to expose you to! What I have written you may relate to it but it was specific to me. God desires to speak directly to you and about what he wants to do through you and in you; he is waiting for you to sup with him, waiting for you to pay attention to what he wants to say to you. God desires to bless you, to keep you, to prosper you and not to harm you, to give you hope and a future. (**Jeremiah 29:11**) God desires to protect you from the unseen.... Just as he was waiting on me, he is waiting on YOU!!! He wants to reveal to you the veils that hinder your progress so that he can show you how to TEAR THEM DOWN! My journey does not end here because for the first time ever I see myself as BEAUTIFUL and I am now on a journey Beyond the veil!

Prayer: I encourage you to pray this simple prayer: God, I love you and I know that you have been speaking to me because I am your child. Please open my heart and mind to hear your voice beyond the chaos and the confusion of this world. Make it plain to me that I am hearing from you. Drown out all other voices that I may sup with you and learn for myself what my true purpose is. Oh God, I anticipate your Divine Connections that will help guide me along my journey! It's in Jesus' name I pray. Amen!

Special Thanks: Walking alongside a Prophet is not the easiest thing to do, because you are vulnerable to the things God wants to reveal to you about yourself! This journey could not have gone the way it did without having this powerful, obedient, selfless, sold out man of God by my side. I learn so much about myself! Through the tears, confusion, revelation, the spooky stuff, the ups, and the downs, dying to his own needs he answered the call of duty! PC (Prophet Clinton Chambers) thank you for being obedient to your calling. To nurture me, guide me, pray for me, encourage me, correct me, and Instruct me. There are no words to express my gratitude to you! This was not an easy journey but you didn't give up on me and for that, I say thank you! We need more examples like you in this world!

Thank you, Tiarra Kemp, for seeing the vision I had for my book cover and bringing it to life!

I thank my Pastor and Shepard Reverend Dr. Cynthia L. Hale! She could have never known that three weeks prior to me stepping foot through the doors of Ray Of Hope Christian Church, that I attempted to commit suicide. I spent three days in the belly of a whale called the "Crazy House"/Psychiatric Ward, this was my Jonah experience. But through her leadership, love, transparency, and her example; I became just as strong as she preached and displayed herself to be! I am because she is!!! I thank you for being a part of the beauty within me!

References

Scripture Research from –Bible Gateway - biblegateway.com.

All Baby Names, December 18, 2019, https://www.allbabynames.com/BabyName/Hebrew/Lapidoth.aspx, Page 90.

Some scriptures are quoted from Zondervan NIV Study Bible 2002 Edition